D1563047

THE KUHLMAN-BINET TESTS FOR CHILDREN OF PRESCHOOL AGE

UNIVERSITY OF MINNESOTA
THE INSTITUTE OF CHILD WELFARE
MONOGRAPH SERIES NO. II

THE KUHLMAN-BINET TESTS FOR CHILDREN OF PRESCHOOL AGE

A CRITICAL STUDY AND EVALUATION

By

FLORENCE L. GOODENOUGH, PH.D.

RESEARCH ASSISTANT PROFESSOR
THE INSTITUTE OF CHILD WELFARE

GREENWOOD PRESS, PUBLISHERS
WESTPORT, CONNECTICUT

Library of Congress Cataloging in Publication Data

Goodenough, Florence Laura, 1886-
    The Kuhlman-Binet tests for children of preschool age.

    Reprint of the ed. published by the University of
Minnesota Press, Minneapolis, which was issued as no. 2
of University of Minnesota, Institute of Child Welfare.
Monograph series.
    1. Mental tests. 2. Child study. 3. Kuhlmann,
Frederick, 1876-1941. A handbook of mental tests.
I. Title. II. Series: Minnesota. University.
Institute of Child Development and Welfare. Monograph
series, no. 2.
BF431.G626 1973   153.9'32   73-9226
ISBN 0-8371-6990-9

Originally published in 1928 by the
University of Minnesota Press, Minneapolis

Reprinted with the permission of the University of
Minnesota Press

Reprinted in 1973 by Greenwood Press,
a division of Williamhouse-Regency Inc.

Library of Congress Catalogue Card Number 73-9226

ISBN 0-8371-6990-9

Printed in the United States of America

PREFACE

The problem of the measurement of intelligence in children below the age of six years is of great importance in both its practical and theoretical aspects. In the past, owing to both educational and social demands, interest in intelligence has been concerned largely with the older child, and a considerable body of scientific knowledge and methodology with reference to the standardization and the criteria to be used in intelligence-test measurements has been developed. In the study which is here presented, Dr. Goodenough has applied these scientific criteria in a thoroughgoing and far reaching way to the problem of intelligence testing in young children, and has made a critical evaluation of the tests in the younger years. On reading the monograph, it will become clear that the methods developed in the standardization and evaluation of tests for older children have been applied with scientific rigor to the tests used below the school level and that the techniques and methods have been improved. Dr. Goodenough's work is in many respects a model investigation in the field of intelligence-test evaluation, both with regard to the techniques employed and the results obtained.

The outstanding contributions of this study are to my mind the demonstration of the deficiencies in the scaling of the individual test items and hence the lack of validity of many of the interpretations which are now placed upon shifts of intelligence quotients in the preschool level, and the demonstration that in the young child as well as in the older child and the adult there is a relationship between paternal occupation and intelligence level. Such a relationship found in the older child and in the adult may be explained in part on the basis of environmental factors. The clear demonstration of its existence at the two-year level, prior to the operation of the majority of those environmental factors, is of fundamental significance.

One of the products of this study carried into its next stage will be the development of an intelligence scale for young children equal, from the standpoint of accurate scaling and standardization, to those used at higher ages. With the more accurate measuring instrument, many of the practical and theoretical problems related to mental development can be attacked.

JOHN E. ANDERSON,
Director, Institute of Child Welfare

ACKNOWLEDGMENTS

If I were to undertake to make separate mention of all the persons whose assistance has made this study possible, the list would take up several pages of this book. One of the most serious problems that the worker with children of preschool age has to meet arises through the comparative inaccessibility of the subjects and the consequent difficulty of collecting adequate data based upon a fairly representative sampling of the population. The extent to which this difficulty has been overcome in the present instance is largely due to the interest and cooperation which the Institute has experienced from the time of its organization.

To the superintendents and teachers in the Northeast Neighborhood House, the Pillsbury Settlement House, Unity Settlement House, Margaret Barry House, Emanuel Cohen Center, South Side Neighborhood House, Lutheran Inner Mission, Wells Memorial House, Stevens Avenue Home, and the Children's Home Society, through whose cordial hospitality nearly one-fourth of the cases were made available for study, our indebtedness is very great. The Minneapolis Infant Welfare Society kindly permitted us to examine children at the clinics conducted under its auspices. Grateful acknowledgments are also due to Mrs. Gladys Wolcott of the Minneapolis Children's Protective Society, to the Family Welfare Association, and to the members of the Minneapolis Junior League, through whose volunteer services the children from the Children's Protective Society were brought to the Institute for examination. To the many parents who have contributed so freely of their time and effort, not only in this study but in many others conducted by the Institute, too much credit can hardly be given.

Particular mention should be made of the work of Miss Mildred Buffington (now Mrs. Francis Rich), who acted as research assistant throughout the duration of the study, and whose intelligent collaboration and unflagging enthusiasm contributed materially to the success of the project.

To Dr. John E. Anderson and Dr. Josephine C. Foster I am indebted for many helpful suggestions during the course of the study, and in the preparation of the manuscript Mrs. Margaret Harding has given valuable editorial assistance.

FLORENCE L. GOODENOUGH

MINNEAPOLIS, MINNESOTA
DECEMBER, 1927

CONTENTS

LIST OF TABLES

LIST OF FIGURES

CHAPTER I

THE CONSTANCY OF THE IQ

DISCUSSION OF PREVIOUS FINDINGS.

It is now more than twenty years since Binet published his
first scale for the measurement of intellectual development in
children.[1] Since then a number of revisions and extensions
of the original scale have appeared in this country and
abroad. Binet himself published two revisions[2] of the 1905
scale before his death, both of which were translated into
English by Goddard[3] and his co-workers with such minor
changes as would make the tests suitable for use with Ameri-
can children. Kuhlman published his first revision of the

---

[1] Alfred Binet and Th. Simon, "Méthodes nouvelles pour le diagnostic du niveau intellectuel des anormaux." *L'Année Psychologique*, Vol.
11 (1905), pp. 191-244, and "Application des méthodes nouvelles au
diagnostic du niveau intellectuel chez des enfants normaux et anormaux
d'hospice et d'ecole primaire," *ibid.*, pp. 245-366.

[2] Alfred Binet and Th. Simon, "Le développement de l'intelligence
chez les enfants," *L'Année Psychologique*, Vol. 14 (1908), pp. 1-94;
La mesure du développement de l'intelligence chez les jeunes enfants.
Bulletin de la Société libre pour l'Étude psychologique de l'Enfant.
(1911); *A Method of Measuring the Development of the Intelligence
of Young Children.* Translation by Clara Harrison Town (Vineland,
N. J., 1915).

[3] H. H. Goddard, "The Binet and Simon Tests of Intellectual
Capacity," The *Training School Bulletin*, Vol. 5 (1908), pp. 3-9.

——"A Measuring Scale for Intelligence," *ibid.*, Vol. 6 (1910),
pp. 146-155.

——"Two Thousand Normal Children Measured by the Binet
Measuring Scale of Intelligence," *Pedagogical Seminary*, Vol. 18 (1911),
232-259.

scale in 1912;[4] a second and much extended revision in 1922.[5] In 1915 Yerkes, Bridges, and Hardwick published their Point Scale, which consists of a re-arrangement and extension of the Binet tests, with a different scoring procedure.[6] A revision of this book was published by Yerkes and Foster in 1923.[7] The Stanford Revision by Terman and others appeared in 1916.[8] In America, this form of the scale is still used more extensively than any other. The most recent revision is that by Herring,[9] which, it has been stated by the author, shows a sufficiently high correlation with the Stanford Revision to warrant its use as an alternative form of this test. Revisions of the scale have also been published in several European countries.

During recent years, a considerable body of evidence as to the "constancy" of the IQ has been accumulated. While the reports from different sources vary to some extent, practically all investigators have found that the amount of change from test to test in the IQ level of school children is, under ordinary circumstances, so small as to be of little or no practical sig-

[4] F. Kuhlman, "A Revision of the Binet-Simon System for Measuring the Intelligence of Children," *Journal of Psycho-Asthenics. Monograph Supplement* (September, 1912), 44 pages.

[5] F. Kuhlman, *A Handbook of Mental Tests* (Baltimore: Warwick and York, Inc., 1922), 208 pages.

[6] R. M. Yerkes, J. W. Bridges, and Rose Hardwick, *A Point Scale for Measuring Mental Ability* (Baltimore: Warwick and York, Inc., 1915).

[7] R. M. Yerkes and Josephine Curtis Foster, *A Point Scale for Measuring Mental Ability, 1923 Revision* (Baltimore: Warwick and York, 1923), 219 pages.

[8] Lewis M. Terman, *The Measurement of Intelligence* (Boston: Houghton Mifflin, 1916), 362 pages.

Terman et al., *The Stanford Revision and Extension of the Binet-Simon Scale for Measuring Intelligence* (Baltimore: Warwick and York, 1917), 179 pages.

[9] John P. Herring, *Herring Revision of the Binet-Simon Tests* (Yonkers: World Book Co., 1922).

nificance. Terman reports that the correlation between 426 pairs of retests, made at intervals varying from 1 day to 7 years was +.933; that the central tendency of change in IQ was toward a gain of 1.7 points; and that the probable error of a prediction based on the first test was 4.5 points in terms of IQ.[10] These findings have been in general substantiated by other workers, both for school children and for feeble-minded adults in institutions.[11]

Until the past few years, however, little or no experimental evidence has been available by which the constancy of the IQ ratings obtained during the preschool period might be estimated. It has been tacitly assumed by the majority of workers that the tests have approximately equal reliability over the entire range of the scale, in which case the IQ ratings obtained for preschool-age children would be expected to afford as accurate predictions of later mental growth as those obtained for older children. With the recent growth of interest in the young child, a number of studies have, however, appeared which point the need for further investigation into the soundness of this assumption. The greater number of these reports are based upon the records of children enrolled in nursery schools, and for this reason, together with the fact that the population of these schools consists largely of children from the superior social classes, the general applicability of the findings has yet to be established.

Taken at their face value they reveal two notable characteristics. With these young children there appears to be a definite tendency toward a positive change in the IQ rating earned on the second examination as compared with the first,

[10] Lewis M. Terman, *The Intelligence of School Children* (Boston: Houghton Mifflin, 1919), 317 pages.

[11] F. Kuhlman, "Results of Repeated Mental Re-examination of 639 Feebleminded over a period of ten years," *Journal of Applied Psychology*, Vol. 5 (1921), pp. 195-224.

and the gross variability of the IQ itself, as indicated by a comparison of first test with retest, is distinctly greater than that commonly reported for children of school age. Terman's figures show that of 99 children first tested before the age of six, 14.1 per cent showed a change of 15 points or more on retest, while of 336 cases first examined after the age of six only 4.7 per cent varied to this extent.[12] Baldwin and Stecher found that of 59 children first examined between the ages of two and five years, who were given two examinations at intervals varying from three to twenty months, 13 showed a negative and 44 a positive change, while in 2 cases the results were the same on both occasions. The mean amount of change is not stated, but in 22 cases the change was less than 5 points, while 10 cases showed a change of 15 points or more. Thirteen children had had five successive examinations. Of these, four showed a decrease in IQ from the first to the fifth examination of 1 to 6 points. Nine showed an increase of 5 to 33 points. For these thirteen children the average percentage of change from the first to the second examination was 11.8 points.[13]

Baldwin comments on these results as follows:

"The later IQs are in general higher than the first ones, reflecting habituation to experimental conditions, practice, increased facility in the use of language, and mental stimulation resulting from the laboratory activities. In some cases the increase in mental age is so great as to give the impression that the child has actually increased in intelligence. A fairer interpretation would be that the first examination did not actually represent the child's intelligence, or that the favorable environment had developed the potential mental ability

[12] Terman, *Intelligence of School Children.*

[13] Bird Baldwin, and Lorle Stecher, *The Psychology of Pre-School Children* (New York: D. Appleton and Co., 1925), 305 pages.

of the young child. This actual, demonstrable increase in mental status is an argument for giving the young child such opportunity for mental growth."[14]

If the numerical data upon which the premise contained in the sentence last quoted may be interpreted to mean "an actual . . . . increase in mental status" of the children under consideration, and not simply "habituation to experimental conditions," if it can be demonstrated that each of the tests affords an adequate measure of the child's true mental status at the time of testing, and if, furthermore, it can be shown that the advantage thus gained is relatively permanent, and not merely a premature acquisition of superficial accomplishments, then it must be conceded that results such as those just quoted form an extremely strong argument in favor of special training for the child of preschool age.

The findings of other workers with preschool children closely approximate those reported from Iowa. Johnson presents data that give evidence of a "decided lack of constancy in the Intelligence Quotients for young children. The range of actual differences for 125 children who were retested was from 0 to 32 points. Considering the direction of difference the points ranged from —17 to +32. The differences between the first and second tests for the group of 125 children show that there was no change in Intelligence Quotients for nine, or 7 per cent of the cases; a loss for thirty-four or 27 per cent; a gain for eighty-two, or 66 per cent. Twenty-three cases changed ten or more points, six cases changed twenty or more points. The children who were first tested at three or younger show greater instability on retests, averaging greater gains and losses than the older children. Those who were first tested at seven or older show the greatest sta-

[14] *Ibid.*

bility in Intelligence Quotients." The age range of this group was "with few exceptions" from two to eight years at first testing.[15]

In commenting on these results Johnson remarks that "while a tendency toward constancy in rating is indicated, it is the more important that an analysis be made of the conditions under which inconstancy results. Our finding of such large variations in a group of children under the same school environment and tested by the same examiners from year to year emphasizes the need of analysis of the responses to the separate items and the supplementation of the scale by the addition of other types of performances, especially for the ages below seven, that may not be so greatly influenced by training."

Woolley has reported similar results from her tests of young children in the Merrill-Palmer School. She lays particular stress upon the part which a stimulating environment plays in determining the rate of mental growth during the early years. The study is particularly interesting since she compares the changes in IQ of children in the nursery school with those on the waiting list. She finds that while a marked tendency toward an increase in IQ is characteristic of the nursery children, the outside cases show no constant tendency toward either increase or decrease, but vary about equally in both directions. The data are based upon 43 nursery-school children and 36 outside cases. The two groups are fairly similar with regard to age, which ranged from two and a half to five years. The intervals between the two tests ranged from seven to fourteen months in both instances. Mrs. Woolley states that the groups are also similar with respect to home

---

[15] Buford Johnson, *Mental Growth of Children in Relation to the Rate of Growth in Bodily Development* (New York: E. P. Dutton and Co., 1925), 160 pages. See pp. 79-90.

conditions and social status. The amount of change reported, especially for the nursery-school group, is greater than has ordinarily been found by other workers: 33 per cent showed an increase of 20 or more points, as compared to 6 per cent of the waiting list cases. The variation in the IQs obtained for the Merrill-Palmer waiting-list children was less than that for the nursery children, but it also was rather greater than has been found by the other workers who have been quoted.[16]

Several possible explanations may be cited by way of accounting for these results. The theoretical basis of the IQ requires that one of two conditions be met if the IQ is to remain constant. Freeman has expressed these conditions as follows: In Case 1, the yearly increments of growth are equal, but the spread of the distribution in the succeeding years increases uniformly and proportionately. It is further assumed that the growth curves have their origin at birth. In Case 2, the distribution of the scores from year to year remains constant, but the successive yearly increments decrease from age to age according to a logarithmic series.[17] An implication of either condition is that the individual tests at the lower age-levels shall have a far greater degree of reliability than those at the upper age-levels, since success or failure on a single point affects the IQ rating in an inverse ratio to the chronological age. An alternative would be to provide a proportionately greater number of tests for the lower age-levels, but this has not been done in any of the scales thus far published. The effect of unequal overlapping at different ages or with different tests upon the IQ ratings has been noted by

[16] Helen T. Woolley, "The Validity of Standards of Mental Measurement in Young Childhood," *School and Society*, Vol. 21, pp. 476-482.

[17] Frank N. Freeman, *Mental tests, their history, principles, and applications* (Boston: Houghton Mifflin, 1926). See pp. 277-279.

Franzen,[18] Rand,[19] Willson,[20] and others. Among other possible sources of error in the test itself may be mentioned incorrect standardization, resulting in varying difficulty at different age-levels, and lack of objectivity in the directions for giving or scoring the separate items.

A second explanation in some degree allied to the first is the possibility that variations in the IQ as obtained from time to time may represent actual temporary fluctuations in the rate of mental progress. While the weight of evidence thus far obtained has not tended to confirm this hypothesis, it must be remembered that the method of computing the IQ produces an artificial smoothing of the mental growth curve and thus tends to mask whatever individual irregularities may be present. At the upper age-levels this tendency is very marked, but with young children the smoothing process is less effective, and individual fluctuations show up more prominently. If a child of twelve years who has previously tested at 100 fails to make any measurable gain in mental growth over a six-months period, the loss in IQ is only 4 points, but if the same thing occurs with a child of three, the IQ loss will be 13 points. We are not here concerned with the question of the comparative significance of such fluctuations at different ages. The point to be emphasized is that the IQ technique is not well suited to determine their existence in the absence of a more precise measuring instrument than those at present available.

Rand has reported the case of a negro boy first tested at the age of 12 years, 8 months, with an IQ of 58 and retested annually over a period of 5 years. Immediately after the

[18] Raymond Franzen, "Statistical Issues, Sec. I. Commensuration and Age," *Journal of Educational Psychology*, Vol. 15 (1924), pp. 270-73.

[19] Gertrude Rand, "A Discussion of the Quotient Method of Specifying Test Results," *Journal of Educational Psychology*, Vol. 16 (1926), pp. 599-618.

[20] G. M. Willson, "Standard Deviation versus Age as a Score Unit," *Journal of Educational Research*, Vol. 13 (1926), pp. 189-196.

first test he was placed in a special class for backward children where he could be given more adequate educational opportunity. Concerning this case Rand comments as follows:
"The mental age increased on an average of 10 months per
year through the range of chronological age of 12 years, 8
months, to 16 years, 6 months: that is, the boy was progress-
ing along the 83 instead of the 60 IQ level, yet the average
gain in quotient during this period was only 1 point.[21] . . . .
I am unable to say how much of the increase in mental age
was due to practice effect or how much to the effect of adequate schooling for his intelligence. The point I wish to
make here is that the significant increase in the boy's mental
age is obscured by the quotient method of specification because of the magnitude of the denominator of the fraction,
i.e., his chronological age."[22]

While one is hardly justified in assuming that cases such as
this are necessarily due to variation in actual rate of mental
growth rather than to inaccuracies in the measuring instrument, they point the need for further investigation of the
question, especially at the early age-levels, and with reference
to such possible disturbing factors as physical illness, radical
changes in environmental stimulation, etc.

A third explanation is to be found in varying emotional attitudes in the child himself at the time of testing. It is entirely conceivable that factors of an emotional nature may
affect the performance of little children to a much more marked degree than is likely to be the case with older children,
since emotional control ordinarily increases with age. The effect
of emotional factors should be studied, not only with reference
to the subjective observation of emotional attitudes as express-

[21] A better way of stating this would be to compare the lowest and
the highest of the five IQs, since the comparison of an absolute with a
relative change is of doubtful validity. The lowest IQ was 58; the
highest, 63. (F. L. G.).

[22] J. of Educ. Psychol., Vol. 16, pp. 611-12.

ed in behavior during the test, but also with regard to the effect of the personality relationships between child and examiner as indicated by the results obtained by different examiners for the same child, by a comparison of tests made under different surroundings, at different hours of the day (to check up on the effect of irritability due to fatigue, etc.).

In the following chapters, an account will be presented of a study designed to throw light upon certain of the facts which have been discussed. The work was carried out at the Institute of Child Welfare, University of Minnesota, during the year 1925-1926.

SUMMARY

1. Under ordinary conditions, the IQ of school children as determined by an individual Binet test remains relatively constant over periods of several years.

2. While a similar tendency to constancy of the IQ has been established for children of preschool age, the likelihood of variation is decidedly greater than has been found to be the case with older children.

3. There is some indication that the degree of environmental stimulation may be a factor in determining the results of an intelligence test in the case of young children. Data are wanting to show whether apparent acceleration brought about in this way has any lasting effect upon mental development.

4. Theoretical causative factors for the comparative unreliability of the IQs obtained for preschool-age children have been discussed under three main heads: (1) unreliability of the measuring instrument itself; (2) actual fluctuations in the rate of mental growth, presumably occurring as a result of variation in environmental stimulation; (3) varying emotional factors or attitudes in the child which may temporarily inhibit his test performance. In presenting the results of the study under consideration, each of these factors will be taken up separately.

CHAPTER II

EXPERIMENTAL PROCEDURE

PURPOSE

The purpose of the study about to be described was discussed in the preceding chapter. It may be recapitulated briefly as follows: first, to secure further data on the reliability of the Binet tests for children of preschool age, and secondly, to make an experimental investigation into certain theoretical reasons for their unreliability. Incidentally, the material which has been collected has been found to contribute to the study of other related problems, which will be described elsewhere.

TESTS USED

The Stanford Revision is hardly suitable for the generality of children below the age of five years, since no mental-age standards for the ages below three have been derived, and the three-year norms are based upon the examination of only ten children. It should be noted in this connection that in his presentation of the statistical data upon which the test is based, Terman is careful to limit his conclusions to "children between the ages of five and thirteen." Because of these limitations of the Stanford Revision, the Kuhlman 1922 Revision, which includes tests for children of three months and upward, was used. However, since many of the tests for the ages above two years are identical with those of the Stanford Revision, while others are closely similar or differ only in regard to the age-level at which they have been placed, the results obtained may properly be said to have some bearing on the reliability of the Stanford Revision as well.

In the absence of a second form of the test[1] the usual method of determining reliability could not be used. The children were therefore re-examined after an interval of a few weeks (for distribution of intervals, see Table 4), and the results of the two tests were compared, both as to total rating and success or failure on the individual tests.

SUBJECTS

A total of 495 children, ranging in age from 18 to 54 months, were given at least one examination.[2] Of these, 393 were given two examinations as stated above. From these, three groups of 100 children each, whose chronological ages (taken to the nearest birthday) were two, three, and four years respectively were selected for intensive study. This group will hereafter be referred to as the *main experimental group*. The selection was made according to the following criteria:

1. *Paternal occupation.*—The census report[3] on occupations of adult males in Minneapolis was consulted, and the occupations therein listed were grouped into six main categories,[4] using the Barr Scale for Occupational Intelligence and the Taussig industrial classification as guides.[5] The proportion of males between the ages of 21 and 45 years falling within each of these categories was then computed, and an attempt was made to match the proportions thus found as closely as possible.

[1] The Herring Revision mentioned in the preceding chapter is not adapted to the examination of children below the age of five years.

[2] This includes 20 cases in which the attempt to test was unsatisfactory or a complete failure.

[3] Report of the Fourteenth Census of the United States, 1920, Vol. 4. See Table 2, pp. 1144-46.

[4] See Appendix A.

[5] Described in *Genetic Studies of Genius* by Terman et al. (Stanford University Press, 1925). See Vol. 1, pp. 66-72.

2. *Sex.*—Each age group was made up of exactly 50 boys and 50 girls.

3. *Examiners.*—Two examiners, the writer and Miss Mildred Buffington, research assistant in the Institute, made all the tests. In each age group, 25 of the children were tested by the writer on both occasions, 25 were tested by Miss Buffington on both occasions, 25 were tested first by the writer, then by Miss Buffington, and the remaining 25 were tested first by Miss Buffington, then by the writer.

4. *Interval between tests.*—Because of weather conditions, temporary illnesses and the like, it was found to be impossible to hold to an exact interval between the tests. However, an attempt was made to keep the interval within the limits of 4 to 7 weeks (time taken to the nearest week). The exact distribution of intervals is shown in Table 4.

5. *Degree of cooperativeness shown by child during tests.*—In some cases[6] the results of one or both tests were unsatisfactory, either because of language handicap or because of marked shyness or negativism on the part of the child, with which the examiner was unable to cope successfully. Only those cases in which a satisfactory degree of cooperation was secured have been included in the main experimental group.

The 380 cases who were given two satisfactory tests, including the main experimental group and 80 additional cases who failed to meet one or another of the first four criteria mentioned above, will be called the *total retest group.*

The *total group* includes all cases in which an attempt at testing was made, regardless of whether the test was satisfactory or whether a retest was secured.

[6] This includes 20 of the 495 first tests, 13 of the second tests.

SOURCES OF SUPPLY

The children were obtained from the following sources:

1. By voluntary application of parents, either for admission to the nursery school or for the home study group. These children were brought to the Institute laboratory for examination.

2. By home visit made by a member of the Institute staff, and invitation to have child considered a candidate for the nursery school, or, if parents preferred, for the home study group. In order to obtain a suitable distribution of candidates for the nursery school, a rough canvass of that part of the city lying within reasonable transportation distance from the Institute was made according to the following plan: The files of one of the daily papers were consulted for birth records of suitable date. A working list of 168 names of cases then residing in the section of the city under consideration was prepared, and the current issue of the city directory was consulted in order to verify the addresses. Calls were made at these homes,[7] the purpose of the Institute was explained, and the parents invited to register their children. In the course of the call, the parents were also asked whether they knew of other children of suitable age living in the neighborhood, whose parents might be interested in the project. A number of additional cases were located in this way. These children also were brought to the Institute for examination.

3. Infant Welfare Society Clinics. The Minneapolis Infant Welfare Society maintains a number of free clinics in which children whose parents would be unable to keep them under the continued observation of a private pediatrician are given medical supervision up to the age of four years. The purpose of the clinics is preventive, rather than remedial; the children are brought for examination at stated intervals and no sick

[7] Only 79 of the 168 cases could be located.

children are admitted. While the clinics are free, except for a small registration fee, their services are not limited to the very poor but extend upward through the working and middle classes. These children were examined in a separate room at the clinics.

4. Day nurseries. Children in eight day nurseries connected with various settlement houses in the city were examined. For the most part these were children of working mothers. The examinations were made at the nurseries, a separate room being used for the purpose.

5. A social worker from the Family Welfare Association arranged to have the children of suitable age in the families under her supervision examined. This organization deals for the most part with families in marginal circumstances who are in need of temporary help. The children were brought to the Institute laboratory by the social worker.

6. A number of children under the supervision of the Children's Protective Society were examined. These examinations were as a rule made at the Institute, the children being brought to the laboratory by a social worker. A small number were examined at one of the boarding homes where a room suited to the purpose was available, and in a few instances the examination was made at one of the Infant Welfare Clinics before mentioned.

7. All of the two-, three-, and four-year-old children in a small orphanage were examined. These examinations were made at the orphanage, where a separate room for the purpose was available.

COMPOSITION OF MAIN EXPERIMENTAL GROUP

In selecting the cases for this group, an attempt was made to secure a sampling which would be as nearly as possible representative of the total child population of Minneapolis. The extent to which this attempt was successful may be judged from the tables which follow. It should be noted, however, that no assumption is made here with regard to the extent to which the standards obtained for this group may be applied to the general population elsewhere. Such data as are available indicate that there exist very marked local differences in the distribution of the kind of intelligence which is measured by a Binet test, and that considerable caution should be exercised in utilizing norms derived from a single locality as standards by which to form absolute judgments of widely divergent population-groups. It is believed, however, that the data which follow provide an objective basis for comparison which workers from other localities will find serviceable in determining how far, and in what direction, the standards to be presented later may be expected to diverge from typical groups elsewhere.

One of the best single indications of social and intellectual background for which reliable comparative data are readily available is afforded by the distribution of paternal occupations. Table 1 shows the distribution of paternal occupations[8] for the three hundred children of the main experimental group. The 1920 census figures for the city of Minneapolis are given for comparison.

Racial stock is also a factor which should be considered in the make-up of any group which is supposed to be typical of a given population. Table 2 shows the distribution of cases in the main experimental group according to the country of birth of the parents. The 1920 census figures for the city of Minneapolis are also included in the table.[9]

It will be seen that the percentage of native-born whites is greater among the parents of the children in the main experimental group than among the general adult population

[8] See Appendix A.

[9] Report of the Fourteenth Census of the United States (1920), Vol. 3. See Table 10, pp. 926-931.

TABLE 1

DISTRIBUTION OF CASES BY OCCUPATIONAL GROUPS

Group	Per Cent of Total Adult Male Population of Minneapolis	Fathers of Children in Main Experimental Group											
		Age 2			Age 3			Age 4			Total		
		Boys	Girls	Total	Boys	Girls	Total	Boys	Girls	Total	Boys	Girls	Total
I	5.4	5	2	7	2	4	6	3	3	6	10	9	19
II	6.3	4	3	7	4	3	7	1	6	7	9	12	21
III	37.3	19	18	37	17	20	37	18	21	39	54	59	113
IV	24.3	9	14	23	9	14	23	15	9	24	33	37	70
V	14.9	8	8	16	10	5	15	6	6	12	24	19	43
VI	11.8	5	5	10	8	4	12	7	5	12	20	14	34
Total	100.0	50	50	100	50	50	100	50	50	100	150	150	300

17

TABLE 2

DISTRIBUTION OF CASES BY NATIVITY OF PARENTS
(Main Experimental Group)

	Percentage of Minneapolis Population in 1920		Main Experimental Group					
	Males Ages 25-59	Females Ages 25-49	Age 2		Age 3		Age 4	
			Fathers	Mothers	Fathers	Mothers	Fathers	Mothers
			80	87	75	81	68	84
United States (whites)	61.0	72.2	80	87	75	81	68	84
United States (colored)	1.5	1.2	1	1	1	1	..	..
British Isles	2.7	1.9	2	3	1	2	2	2
Norway	6.8	4.9	1	2	1	..	2	..
Sweden-Denmark	12.1	8.8	3	2	2	2	5	2
Germany	3.0	1.9	1	..	2	..	3	..
Poland	1.9	1.4	1	1	4	5	5	4
Other countries (Central Europe)	1.9	1.4	2	2	1	1	1	..
Russia	2.4	1.9	..	..	4	2	8	4
Other countries (Eastern Europe)	1.1	0.8	3	..	2	2	3	2
Southern Europe	0.7	0.5	2	1	2	2	..	..
Asia (exclusive of Chinese and Japanese)	0.2	0.2	..	..	..	..	..	..
Canada, other American countries	3.1	2.3	3	1	3	2	3	2
Am. Indian, Chinese, Japanese	0.2	0.1	1	..	1	..	..	..
All others, including unknown	1.4	0.5	..	..	1	..	..	..

18

of the city. This is in part due to the fact that children with marked foreign-language handicap were not included. However, an examination of the proportion of children of foreign parentage in the total group shows a similar, though smaller, discrepancy. There are several possible explanations for this fact. It is probable that a larger percentage of unmarried persons will be found among the foreign-born than in the general population. It is also probable that the first-generation foreigners are somewhat less likely than others to avail themselves of the advantages offered by the various social agencies through lack of information either as to their existence or purpose.

FIGURE I

DISTRIBUTION OF CASES ACCORDING TO SOURCE OF SUPPLY

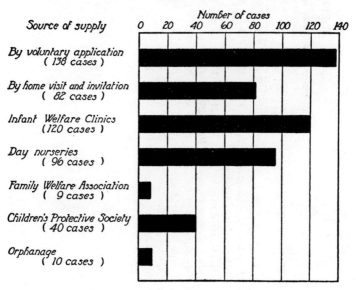

TABLE 3

DISTRIBUTION OF CASES BY SOURCE OF SUPPLY
(Main Experimental Group)

	Age 2			Age 3			Age 4			Totals		
	Boys	Girls	Total	Boys	Girls	Total	Boys	Girls	Total	Boys	Girls	Total
1. By voluntary application	16	7	23	14	15	29	14	12	26	44	34	78
2. By home visit and invitation (University district)	7	11	18	6	5	11	6	10	16	19	26	45
3. Infant Welfare Clinics	16	25	41	7	15	22	8	5	13	31	45	76
4. Day Nurseries	7	3	10	14	9	23	12	16	28	33	28	61
5. Family Welfare Assn.	0	2	2	2	1	3	1	1	2	3	4	7
6. Children's Protective Soc.	4	1	5	4	3	7	7	6	13	15	10	25
7. Orphanage	0	1	1	3	2	5	2	0	2	5	3	8
Total	50	50	100	50	50	100	50	50	100	150	150	300

A third important selective factor lies in the sources from which the cases are drawn. The nature of the sources from which the children used in this study were obtained was described in a preceding section. Table 3 and Figure I show the proportion of cases in the main experimental group obtained from each of the seven sources mentioned. The relationship between source of supply and paternal occupation is shown graphically in Figure II.

All the cases in Group I and all except three of the cases in Group II have been obtained either by voluntary application or by home visits within the university district. These two sources combined furnish more than four times their normal quota of cases belonging to the two upper occupational classes, and only a little more than one-fifth the normal proportion of cases belonging to the two lowest groups. Except for the absence of children belonging to the professional classes, the Infant Welfare Clinics provide a more nearly representative group than any other single source. The remaining four sources are all over-weighted at the lower end of the scale.

It will be recalled that the main experimental group constitutes a selection from the total group of 495 cases who were examined. This selective factor was in part controlled, but in some respects it constituted an uncontrollable element in the situation. In order to ascertain as far as possible what part the uncontrollable factors may have played in determining the final distribution of cases, an analysis of the "turnover" (cases not included in the main experimental group) was undertaken. Figure III shows the results according to source of supply. Figure IV shows the same facts in relation to paternal occupation.

FIGURE II

RELATIONSHIP BETWEEN PATERNAL OCCUPATION AND SOURCE OF SUPPLY

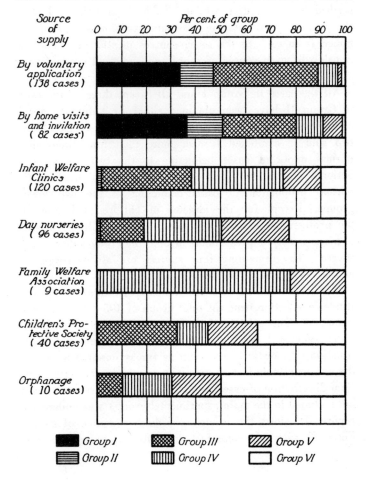

FIGURE III

ANALYSIS OF TURNOVER BY SOURCE OF SUPPLY

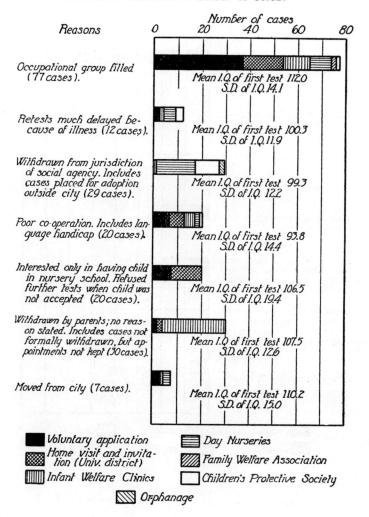

FIGURE IV

ANALYSIS OF TURNOVER BY PATERNAL OCCUPATION

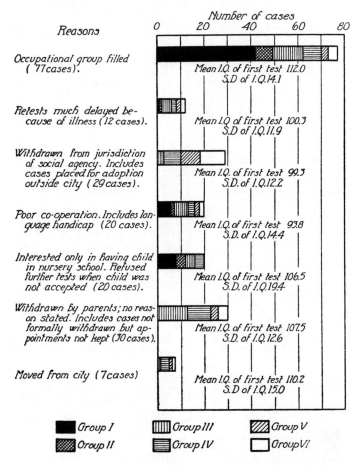

It will be seen that more children have been eliminated in order to make the group conform to the standard distribution of paternal occupations than for any other one reason. Nearly all these cases belong to the upper occupational groups and they are found chiefly among the voluntary applicants. The next most important source of elimination is to be found almost entirely among the cases obtained at the Infant Welfare Society clinics. Since the periodic clinic examinations for children at these ages occur at intervals varying from three to six months, our second examination involved an additional visit to the clinics. Many of the mothers failed to keep the appointment for this test. The third important source of elimination comes from the shifting population in the day nurseries and the Children's Protective Society. Such shifts are of characteristic occurrence in these organizations, and there is no reason for believing that those cases for whom the transfer chanced to occur during the interval between tests differ in any essential respect from the generality of the cases which they handle.

A comparison of the mean IQs of the cases eliminated with those of the totals for corresponding sources of supply and occupational levels shows no significant differences except for the cases whose cooperation during the test situation was unsatisfactory. These tend to run low, as was to be expected. It appears, therefore, that the most important effect of selection has been to secure a more nearly representative group through the elimination of the excess cases at the upper occupational levels. Further data on this subject will be presented in the following chapter.

The facts presented in the foregoing tables indicate in some measure the extent to which the attempt to secure a representative group of cases for the main study was successful. There are, however, other factors which may have affected the selection to some extent, and which the nature of the experiment does not permit us to gauge. There is some reason for believing that both occupational extremes have been somewhat exaggerated, since the professional group is made up very largely of the children of university faculty members, while the lower occupational levels were recruited largely from the more incompetent members of their class. It is impossible to say to what extent these opposed factors have served to balance each other as far as the mean performance of the group is concerned, but it is highly probable that the variability is on this account somewhat greater than would be found for a truly representative sampling of the population of the city.

EXPERIMENTAL CONDITIONS

The distribution of intervals between the two tests for the main experimental group is shown in Table 4. It will be noted that 87.3 per cent of the cases in this group were retested within an interval ranging from 4 to 7 weeks. The effect of length of interval between tests upon changes in the IQ will be discussed in a later chapter.

All examinations were made in a separate room where freedom from interruption could be assured. An attempt was made to schedule all tests at such an hour that the child's daily routine would be interfered with as little as possible; e.g., children accustomed to afternoon naps were examined in the morning or in the late afternoon after they had awakened. However, it sometimes happened that a parent preferred to bring the child in the early afternoon as a time of greater convenience to herself, regardless of the nap period, and several of the Infant Welfare Clinics were held only in the afternoon. The rule, therefore, could not be strictly adhered to in all cases. The question of possible diurnal variation in test performance will be taken up in a later section.

TABLE 4

INTERVAL BETWEEN TESTS BY AGE AND SEX GROUPS
(Main Experimental Group)

Interval (nearest week)	Age 2			Age 3			Age 4			Total
	Boys	Girls	Total	Boys	Girls	Total	Boys	Girls	Total	
4 weeks	9	12	21	7	9	16	9	7	16	53
5 weeks	15	13	28	11	18	29	18	9	27	84
6 weeks	13	10	23	19	11	30	12	23	35	88
7 weeks	6	8	14	5	8	13	4	6	10	37
8 weeks	2	2	4	5	0	5	4	1	5	14
9 weeks	2	4	6	2	2	4	2	1	3	13
10 weeks	0	1	1	1	2	3	1	3	4	8
11 weeks	2	0	2	0	0	0	0	0	0	2
12 weeks	0	0	0	0	0	0	0	0	0	0
13 weeks	1	0	1	0	0	0	0	0	0	1
Total	50	50	100	50	50	100	50	50	100	300

27

In the great majority of cases, no one except the child and the examiner was permitted to be present during the test. In a few instances, especially among the two-year-olds, it seemed advisable to permit the mother to remain in the room if the child seemed worried or anxious without her. This was especially likely to be the case at the Infant Welfare Clinics where the general surroundings were often rather intimidating to a shy or nervous child. Even there, however, it was in most instances possible to have the mother leave the room after a few minutes. Some evidence as to the effect of the mother's presence upon test results will be presented later.

TEST PROCEDURE

One of the chief problems which confronts the examiner of young children has to do with the management of the child before and during the tests. That the child must be put at ease before the test is begun, and that a spirit of interest must be maintained throughout is practically a truism, but few people who have not had extensive experience in the examination of young children realize how much more difficult it is to secure and maintain such an attitude with preschool-age children than is the case with older children. For this reason, a few notes as to the methods that have been found most effective in dealing with children at these early ages during the test situation will not be out of place here.

1. *Reception of child and parent.*—On their arrival at the laboratory, the mother and child are ordinarily received by the examiner rather than by a third person, as this is less disturbing to a shy or timid child. It has been found best to direct the greeting toward the mother rather than toward the child, not only in order to avoid embarrassment on his part, but also because many parents are inclined to seize upon the occasion as an opportunity to show off the child's

social training, and to insist upon his responding at once according to form, a procedure which all too frequently results in the setting up of a negativistic attitude at the start. If the child can be kept in the background until he has had time to adjust to the new situation, one of the main sources of difficulty will be removed. The examiner must, therefore, take care to prevent the mother from making the child the center of attention.

Our procedure has been as follows: The mother is greeted cordially but quietly, and after a single "Good morning, Billy," or equivalent phrase spoken in a casual tone to the child, the mother is at once engaged in conversation on everyday topics which are entirely unrelated to the child. The examiner is careful to avoid approaching too closely to the child at first, and nothing in the nature of fondling or petting is attempted.

After wraps have been removed, both mother and child are invited to come to the examining room where a few attractive toys not used in the tests are placed where the child can see them. If he shows interest in them at once, it has usually been found safe to suggest that he may remain and play with them for a while, and that mother would be more comfortable in the next room. An unusually friendly child may sometimes be taken to the examining room directly without being accompanied by the mother, but if there is any doubt as to his attitude, it is better to follow the procedure outlined.

If the child still appears shy after reaching the examining room, it has been found best not to send the mother away at once. In such cases, both mother and child are seated in the examining room, a small chair being provided for the child beside that of the mother. Neither the examiner nor the mother should urge the child to respond; he should be allowed to take the initiative himself as much as possible, and his behavior must not be commented upon in any way. Under these circumstances, we have found that nearly all children soon begin to show interest in their surroundings, and to volunteer conversation. When this stage has been reached, a toy may be offered, and after it has been accepted and played with for a moment or two, the mother may be sent from the room. In rare cases, most often with the two-year-olds, it may be necessary to permit the mother to remain in the room during the tests, provided she can be induced to remain a quiet and inconspicuous observer.

In the present experiment the tests have been given with the child seated at a low table placed at the left of the examiner's desk, which has a single pedestal at the right. This makes it possible to keep all materials convenient to the examiner's hand, and at the same time out of the child's sight, so that they do not serve as a distraction. Toys and such miscellaneous apparatus as coins, weights, etc., are kept in a drawer at the right. The cards used for the Binet are kept in a specially prepared envelope file,[10] which is placed on the right-hand side of the desk. This arrangement has been found to be exceptionally convenient, a point which is of considerable importance in the examination of young children, for whom it is essential that the test proceed smoothly and at a rather rapid rate if attention is to be sustained throughout.

Before proceeding to the Kuhlman, the Wallin Peg Boards,[11] Series A-D inclusive, have been given in all cases. The results from this test are presented elsewhere.[12]

[10] See Appendix B.

[11] J. E. W. Wallin, "The Peg Form Boards," *Psychological Clinic*, Vol. 12 (1918), pp. 40-53.

[12] Florence L. Goodenough, "The Reliability and Validity of the Wallin Peg Boards," *Psychological Clinic*, October, 1927, pp. 199-215.

The procedure used for the Kuhlman will not be described in detail, since it is for the most part identical with that outlined in the manual which has been referred to. However, a few minor departures from the standardized instructions have been made for certain tests. These are as follows:

Eighteen-months series.—Tests 1, 2, and 4 have been credited on the basis of the mother's report in all cases.

Two-year series.—Test 2 (imitation of movements) has been found to be especially likely to arouse negativism, even in the case of children who respond to other tests without hesitation. We have found that by reversing the order of this and the following test, i.e., giving test 3 before test 2, co-operation can be secured much more readily, since the difficulty with test 2 appears to lie chiefly in its tendency to arouse self-consciousness and test 3 is especially well suited to divert the child's attention from himself. For the best results, test 2 should follow test 3 immediately without any intermediate pause for record-taking.

Test 5. Many of our two-year-old subjects have never been permitted to taste candy or lump sugar. If the test is given according to the standardized method, the incentive varies greatly according to the child's past experience. We have substituted a small telegraph snapper, which is first snapped two or three times while the child looks on, then wrapped and handed to him with the instruction, "See if you can make it snap like that." The procedure is repeated once if the child fails on the first test, and is counted as passed if the child unwraps it on either trial.

Three-year series.—Test 1. We have followed the plan of using the stimulus question for test VII 1 in all cases. Since Binet's time it has been realized that the two questions tend to bring out quite different types of response, but no one seems to have ascertained whether or not the second question is equally effective in evoking description when the pictures are shown a second time, after the child has already responded to them in terms of the earlier stimulus. It is the writer's opinion that a considerable element of error is introduced by the usual method, since the situation for the child who has been given the three-year test and later on has to be given the seven-year form is obviously quite different from that in which the seven-year question is used alone, as is the case with children who earn a basal year of four or more. Our method has therefore been to present the pictures, using the seven-year stimulus question first in all cases, repeating the directions if necessary, and to use the three-year question only in case the seven-year form fails to elicit any kind of a response. The test is then scored for both years simultaneously and is not repeated in the seven-year series. Our results indicate that the placing of descriptive responses at the seven-year level is in part an artifact due to the procedure employed, which has tended to suggest enumeration rather than description in the case of the younger children.

Test III 2 is another which frequently provokes negativism through arousing self-consciousness. We have used a small doll for this test and have asked the child to point out its features rather than his own. This completely overcomes the difficulty in practically all instances, and in this form the test becomes one of the most popular in the entire series.

Tests III 4 and III 6 are also likely to present some difficulties since they have little intrinsic interest for the child. We have employed a number of devices for arousing interest in these and other similar tests in the scale. A pair of toy telephones, one of which the examiner uses while the other is given to the child, is sometimes very effective. A mild kind of bribery, taking the form of, "Now I'll see if you can say something for me, and then we'll see what I have in this box," is also useful. It is better not to press the point if antagonism is encountered, but to pass on to something else and return to it later, as too much urging often defeats its own purpose and may arouse an unfavorable attitude toward the whole situation, which carries over to other tests.

Four-year series.—These tests have been given according to the manual, except that in cases of very marked failure on III 8, IV 5 has not been given, and if a child fails to discriminate between any of the forms in IV 4, IV 6 has also been omitted.

Five-year series.—No changes.

Six-year series.—No changes except that VI 6 has not been given to children whose oral counting in test V 1 (disregarding answer to the "How many?" question) was incorrect.

Seven-year series.—The change in VII 1 was noted under III 1. No other changes have been made except that VII 8 has not been given in case of complete failure on V 2.

Eight-year series.—Tests VIII 1, VIII 3, and VIII 8 have not been given to children who failed on V 1. Test VIII 7 has not been given to children who made a complete failure on VI 7. In cases of marginal failure on VI 7, VIII 7 has also been tried.

Nine-year series.—Tests IX 4 and IX 8 have not been given to children who failed on V 1.

None of the subjects succeeded with any of the nine-year tests, hence the ten-year series has not been given.

The usual limits of complete testing, which require the establishment of a basal year in which all the tests are passed, and continuation until a year is reached in which all tests are failed, has been followed in all cases.

In general the tests have been given in the order recommended in the manual. However it has sometimes been found necessary to depart from this order to some degree in order to secure maximum cooperation on the part of the child. While it is true that such changes in order of procedure are in themselves undesirable, since the mental set of the child may be somewhat affected thereby, it is equally true that a Binet test with a young child rarely approaches the highly standardized situation which is possible with older children or with adults. At these early ages the attention is extremely fleeting, and unless a sound-proof room without any sort of visual stimuli present—an obvious impossibility—could be provided, distractions which interfere with the mental set are bound to creep in. The normally alert three-year-old, if he is entirely at his ease, is likely to interrupt the formal test procedure with all sorts of confidences; he remembers his new shoes and these must be admired at once, a whistle from a passing train requires explanation, he needs to visit the toilet, etc., etc. It is impossible to repress these comments completely, without danger of losing control of the situation; and it accordingly becomes necessary to recall the child's attention, or make sure that it has not been lost, before presenting each new test. Too rigid an adherence to formal procedure in insisting upon an absolutely constant order of presentation often introduces a greater error than that which it is designed to correct, since it is likely to result in a perfunctory type of response or even complete refusal to cooperate further. Since the fleeting attention of these young children renders the "mental set" a largely uncontrollable factor at best, except for the momentarily imposed conditions of the particular experiment, it has seemed better to depart from the usual order of procedure in those cases where resistance has been encountered at some particular point, and return to the difficulty at a more propitious moment later on. With care in handling the child from the outset, such cases are exceptional, but they occur at times even with the most experienced examiners, and it is not always possible to foresee the point at which they are likely to arise. It is not improbable that many of these particularized resistances have their origin in conditioned reactions previously established.

SUMMARY

1. The experiment under consideration was undertaken with view to securing additional data on the reliability of the Kuhlman-Binet tests for preschool-age children.

2. A total of 495 children ranging in age from 18 to 54 months were given at least one test. Of these, 393 children were retested after an interval of approximately six weeks. From these, three groups of 100 children each, whose ages, taken to the nearest birthday, were 2, 3, and 4 years respectively were selected for intensive study. This group is referred to as the *main experimental group*.

3. In selecting cases for the main experimental group an attempt was made to secure a sampling which would represent the total child population of Minneapolis as nearly as possible. The distribution of occupations of adult males as reported for the city of Minneapolis in the 1920 census was used as a criterion. The complete list of occupations was divided into six main categories on the basis of the Barr Scale for Occupational Intelligence, and the Taussig Industrial Classification. The proportion falling within each group was matched as closely as possible.

4. Racial stock, as indicated by nativity of parents, was also compared with the census report. The proportion of native whites was found to be in excess of that reported for the general population of the city. Possible explanations for this discrepancy are discussed.

5. Exactly 50 boys and 50 girls were included at each age.

6. The testing was done by two examiners. In each age group 25 of the cases were tested by Examiner A on both occasions, 25 by Examiner B on both occasions, 25 were tested first by Examiner A, then by Examiner B, and 25 first by Examiner B, then by Examiner A.

7. Cases were obtained from seven different sources as follows: Of the total group of 495, 138 from voluntary ap-

plications, 82 by home visit and invitation, 120 from Infant Welfare Clinics, 96 from day nurseries, 9 from the Family Welfare Association, 40 from the Children's Protective Society, and 10 from an orphanage. A high correlation was found to exist between source of supply and paternal occupation.

8. An analysis of the cases not included in the main experimental group justifies the belief that the selection has resulted in the formation of a group which is reasonably representative of the child population of Minneapolis. A comparison of the data presented in this and the following chapters with corresponding conditions elsewhere will provide a basis for determining with greater precision than would otherwise be possible, how far and in what direction the standards derived from this group may be expected to diverge from those obtained from typical groups in other localities.

9. A description of the experimental conditions and the general test procedure is presented, with particular attention to methods which have been found useful in securing the maximum degree of cooperation on the part of the child.

10. A few minor departures from the standardized instructions for administering the tests have been made. These are specifically noted and described.

CHAPTER III

ANALYSIS OF RESULTS: THE SCALE AS A WHOLE

Certain theoretical reasons for the inconstancy of the IQ as obtained by retests were discussed in Chapter I. These reasons were grouped under three main heads as follows:

1. Unreliability of the measuring instrument.

2. Actual fluctuations in the rate of mental growth, presumably occurring as a result of variations in environmental stimulation.

3. Varying emotional attitudes in the child.

Unreliability of the measuring instrument may be the result of a number of different causes. Since the scale is expressed in terms of relative rather than absolute measures, any irregularities in the composition of the age groups upon which the original standardization was based may be expected to result in corresponding irregularities in the individual measurements which are derived by comparison with these standards. Unreliability also results from lack of objectivity in methods of giving and scoring the tests, effect of practice or of specific coaching in individual cases, and similar adventitious factors.

In this chapter an attempt will be made to show to what extent the factors just mentioned affect the reliability of the scale as a whole. The reliability of the individual test items will be considered in the following chapter.

VALIDITY OF AGE NORMS

Norms derived from the main experimental group.—Table 5 shows the means and standard deviations of chronological ages at the time of the first test for the main experimental

TABLE 5
MEANS AND STANDARD DEVIATIONS OF CHRONOLOGICAL AGE GROUPS BY SEX*
(Main Experimental Group)

	Age 2			Age 3			Age 4		
	Boys	Girls	Total	Boys	Girls	Total	Boys	Girls	Total
Mean	2-0.0	1-11.8	1-11.9	2-11.3	2-11.3	2-11.3	4-0.2	4-0.1	4-0.1
S.D.	3.8	3.4	3.5	3.8	3.2	3.5	3.5	3.6	3.5

*Age at time of first test, expressed in years and months.

TABLE 6
DISTRIBUTION OF MENTAL AGES EARNED ON FIRST TEST BY AGE AND SEX
(Main Experimental Group)

	Age 2			Age 3			Age 4		
	Boys	Girls	Total	Boys	Girls	Total	Boys	Girls	Total
6-3 — 6-5	....	....	....	....	....	....	....	....	....
6-0 — 6-2	....	....	....	....	....	....	....	1	1
5-9 — 5-11	....	....	....	....	....	....	....	2	2
5-6 — 5-8	....	....	....	....	....	....	1	2	3
5-3 — 5-5	....	....	....	....	....	....	5	5	10
5-0 — 5-2	....	....	....	....	....	....	1	7	8
4-9 — 4-11	....	....	....	1	....	1	4	9	13
4-6 — 4-8	....	....	....	....	....	....	7	3	10
4-3 — 4-5	....	....	....	1	7	8	5	4	9
4-0 — 4-2	....	....	....	1	5	6	10	3	13
3-9 — 3-11	....	....	....	2	1	3	6	7	13
3-6 — 3-8	....	....	....	5	2	7	2	3	5
3-3 — 3-5	....	....	....	5	4	9	6	2	8
3-0 — 3-2	1	0	1	7	9	16	2	2	4
2-9 — 2-11	5	4	9	7	11	18	1	....	1
2-6 — 2-8	7	2	9	12	3	15	....	....	....
2-3 — 2-5	6	9	15	7	3	10	....	....	....
2-0 — 2-2	10	16	26	1	3	4	....	....	....
1-9 — 1-11	7	7	14	0	2	2	....	....	....
1-6 — 1-8	12	11	23	1	0	1	....	....	....
1-3 — 1-5	2	1	3	....	....	....	....	....	....
1-0 — 1-2	....	....	....	....	....	....	....	....	....
Total	50	50	100	50	50	100	50	50	100
Mean	2-1.1	2-0.6	2-0.9	2-11.5	3-2.1	3-0.8	4-2.5	4-6.8	4-4.7
S.D.	5.5	4.5	5.0	7.2	8.7	8.0	8.0	9.0	8.8

TABLE 7

DISTRIBUTION OF MENTAL AGES EARNED ON SECOND TEST BY AGE AND SEX
(Main Experimental Group)

	Age 2			Age 3			Age 4		
	Boys	Girls	Total	Boys	Girls	Total	Boys	Girls	Total
6-3 — 6-5	....	....	....	....	....	....	....	1	1
6-0 — 6-2	....	....	....	....	....	....	1	3	4
5-9 — 5-11	....	....	....	....	....	....	1	4	5
5-6 — 5-8	....	....	....	....	....	....	3	4	7
5-3 — 5-5	....	....	....	....	....	....	2	7	9
5-0 — 5-2	....	....	....	2	....	2	5	12	17
4-9 — 4-11	....	....	....	....	6	6	8	3	11
4-6 — 4-8	....	....	....	2	4	6	10	4	14
4-3 — 4-5	....	....	....	1	5	6	9	4	13
4-0 — 4-2	....	....	....	5	1	6	6	3	9
3-9 — 3-11	....	....	....	2	1	3	2	0	2
3-6 — 3-8	....	....	....	2	2	4	2	2	4
3-3 — 3-5	1	....	1	2	8	10	1	3	4
3-0 — 3-2	2	2	4	12	7	19	....	....	....
2-9 — 2-11	9	3	12	3	7	10	....	....	....
2-6 — 2-8	6	7	13	11	5	16	....	....	....
2-3 — 2-5	11	10	21	6	3	9	....	....	....
2-0 — 2-2	8	12	20	1	....	1	....	....	....
1-9 — 1-11	4	13	17	....	1	1	....	....	....
1-6 — 1-8	8	3	11	....	....	....	....	....	....
1-3 — 1-5	1	....	1	1	....	1	....	....	....
1-0 — 1-2	....	....	....	....	....	....	....	....	....
Total	50	50	100	50	50	100	50	50	100
Mean	2-3.4	2-2.3	2-2.9	3-1.7	3-5.7	3-3.7	4-7.4	4-11.6	4-9.5
S.D.	5.8	4.5	5.2	9.5	10.0	10.0	6.8	8.9	8.2

group. Table 6 shows the distribution of mental ages earned by this group on the first test, and Table 7 of those earned on the second test. Table 8 shows the distribution of IQs earned on the first test, and Table 9 of the IQs earned on the second test.

TABLE 8

DISTRIBUTION BY AGE AND SEX OF IQ EARNED ON FIRST TEST
(Main Experimental Group)

IQ	Age 2			Age 3			Age 4			Total		
	Boys	Girls	Total	Boys	Girls	Total	Boys	Girls	Total	Boys	Girls	Total
160-169	…	…	…	…	…	…	…	…	…	…	…	…
150-159	…	…	…	…	…	…	…	…	…	…	…	…
140-149	…	…	…	…	2	2	1	2	3	1	4	5
130-139	1	2	3	1	7	8	2	8	10	4	17	21
120-129	4	5	9	8	7	15	6	10	16	18	22	40
110-119	16	11	27	7	4	11	8	9	17	31	24	55
100-109	12	14	26	5	14	19	17	10	27	34	38	72
90- 99	8	16	24	16	9	25	7	9	16	31	34	65
80- 89	7	2	9	11	3	14	6	2	8	24	7	31
70- 79	2	…	2	1	2	3	2	…	2	5	2	7
60- 69	…	…	…	1	2	3	1	…	1	2	2	4
50- 59	…	…	…	…	…	…	…	…	…	…	…	…
40- 49	…	…	…	…	…	…	…	…	…	…	…	…
Total	50	50	100	50	50	100	50	50	100	150	150	300
Mean	104.3	105.9	105.1	100.7	108.1	104.4	104.7	114.1	109.4	105.8	109.4	106.3
S.D.	13.8	12.0	13.0	15.9	19.6	18.2	16.2	15.7	16.6	15.4	16.4	16.2

TABLE 9

Distribution by Age and Sex of IQ Earned on Second Test
(Main Experimental Group)

IQ	Age 2 Boys	Age 2 Girls	Age 2 Total	Age 3 Boys	Age 3 Girls	Age 3 Total	Age 4 Boys	Age 4 Girls	Age 4 Total	Total Boys	Total Girls	Total
160-169	...	...	...	...	...	...	...	...	...	...	...	...
150-159	...	...	...	...	2	2	...	1	1	...	3	3
140-149	1	2	3	2	6	8	2	2	4	5	10	15
130-139	5	...	5	4	6	10	4	13	17	13	19	32
120-129	8	4	12	3	5	8	9	7	16	20	16	36
110-119	15	15	30	8	6	14	11	19	30	34	40	74
100-109	6	12	18	9	10	19	16	3	19	31	25	56
90- 99	7	16	23	8	9	17	5	2	7	20	27	47
80- 89	5	1	6	12	4	16	3	3	6	20	8	28
70- 79	2	...	2	3	1	4	...	...	...	5	1	6
60- 69	1	...	1	...	1	1	...	...	...	1	1	2
50- 59	...	...	...	...	...	...	...	...	...	...	...	...
40- 49	...	...	...	1	...	1	...	...	...	1	...	1
Total	50	50	100	50	50	100	50	50	100	150	150	300
Mean	109.1	107.1	108.1	101.9	113.3	107.6	112.1	119.9	116.0	107.7	113.8	110.6
S.D.	17.8	12.6	15.5	20.2	21.7	21.7	14.4	15.3	15.3	18.1	17.7	18.1

41

Tables 5-9 show that the norms obtained by the original standardization are somewhat too easy for this group at each of the three ages studied. Kuhlman's own figures show a similar discrepancy. The mean IQs which he obtained were 108 for his two-year-olds, 106 for his three-year-olds, and 107 for his four-year-olds. Kuhlman states that these high figures are due to the large number of "baby contest" children included. If our group may be regarded as typical of Minneapolis children, it appears that some modification of the original standards in the direction of more stringent requirements is desirable. It will be shown later that incorrect placement of tests at the five and six year age-levels is the main reason both for the exceptionally high ratings of the four-year-old group, and for the high variability of the three-year-olds.

The second ratings are in general higher than the first. This tendency will be discussed in detail in a later section of this chapter.

Sex differences.—On the first test the girls rank somewhat higher than the boys at all ages, and this apparent superiority is maintained on the second test at ages three and four. The differences are in the same direction and approximately equal in amount to those reported by Terman. (See *The Measurement of Intelligence*, p. 69.) While the differences are too small to be of practical significance, the fact that they appear to be as clearly defined among preschool-age children as among children of school age is a matter of fundamental importance. The question of sex differences has been taken up in more detail in a separate study.[1]

Racial stock.—None of the children in this group were foreign-born of foreign stock. The data on racial origin are, therefore, based upon birthplace of parents. The number

[1] Florence L. Goodenough, "The Consistency of Sex Differences in Mental Traits at Various Ages," *Psychological Review*, Vol. 34 (1927), pp. 440-462.

of cases of foreign-born parents is so small that the results can be regarded as suggestive only. They have been summarized briefly in Tables 10 and 11.

TABLE 10

MEANS AND STANDARD DEVIATIONS OF IQ ACCORDING TO NATIVITY OF FATHER
(Total group, omitting unsatisfactory tests; ages and sexes combined)

	First Test			Second Test		
	Cases	Mean	S.D.	Cases	Mean	S.D.
United States (whites)	356	108.0	15.8	291	113.2	18.5
United States (colored)	3	97.8	12.5	2	114.5	2.0
British Isles	10	112.5	17.2	5	110.5	10.2
Norway	6	109.5	15.3	4	114.5	21.2
Sweden-Denmark	21	102.1	12.3	11	109.4	8.9
Germany	11	110.0	13.0	7	118.8	12.9
Poland	12	103.7	14.4	11	104.5	14.1
Other countries (Central Europe)	9	96.7	13.1	7	97.4	16.7
Russia	15	105.8	18.9	13	110.7	17.8
Other countries (Eastern Europe)	9	104.5	14.9	9	107.8	16.3
Southern Europe	5	110.5	17.4	4	114.5	25.5
Asia (exclusive of Chinese and Japanese)	2	109.5	5.0	2	109.5	5.0
Canada, other American countries	12	95.3	18.5	12	101.2	25.3
Am. Indian, Chinese, Japanese	0	....	....	....	....	....
All others, including unknown	4	89.5	5.0	2	89.5	5.0
Totals	475			380		

The question of natio-racial differences in mentality is one which has aroused much interest during the past few years, especially since the publication of the data derived from the army intelligence tests. That certain immigrant groups and their immediate descendants differ greatly in their performance on standard intelligence tests by the time they have arrived at school age has been shown by so many independent workers that, whatever may be its significance, the fact itself can hardly be questioned. Up to the present time, practically no data on this subject derived from the examination of children during the preschool years have appeared. Such a study would be well worth while, since the nearer we approach the point of origin in our studies of behavior, the more adequately can we explain our findings. Kelley[2] has shown that school training has a tendency to decrease, rather than to increase, certain differences previously found among the members of a group. A study of natio-racial differences among children who have not been subjected to the influence of school training might do much to clarify our thinking along these lines. The small amount of data which we have

TABLE 11

MEANS AND STANDARD DEVIATIONS OF IQ ACCORDING TO NATIVITY OF MOTHER
(Total group, omitting unsatisfactory tests; ages and sexes combined)

	First Test			Second Test		
	Cases	Mean	S.D.	Cases	Mean	S.D.
United States (whites)	387	108.1	15.8	319	113.1	18.7
United States (colored)	3	97.8	12.5	2	114.5	2.0
British Isles	10	109.5	14.3	7	111.6	10.3
Norway	2	94.5	3.3	2	84.5	3.3
Sweden-Denmark	21	97.8	10.4	8	109.5	11.2
Germany	4	109.5	11.2	1	124.5	....
Poland	12	103.7	15.5	12	105.3	15.0
Other countries (Central Europe)	7	85.9	12.5	5	78.5	10.2
Russia	9	103.4	19.1	8	104.5	12.2
Other countries (Eastern Europe)	6	104.5	17.3	5	104.5	21.0
Southern Europe	3	114.5	20.0	3	114.5	16.3
Asia (exclusive of Chinese and Japanese)	3	104.5	8.2	3	111.2	14.9
Canada, other American countries	7	104.5	13.1	5	112.5	13.3
Am. Indian, Chinese, Japanese	0	....	....	....	....	....
All others, including unknown	1	94.5	......	..	....	....
Totals	475			380		

[2] T. L. Kelley, *The Effect of Nurture upon Native Differences* (New York: Macmillan Co., 1926).

TABLE 12

MEANS AND STANDARD DEVIATIONS OF IQ RATINGS BY AGE AND PATERNAL OCCUPATION

(Total retest group)

	Age 2			Age 3			Age 4			Total		
	No. cases	Mean	S.D.	No. cases	Mean	S.D.	No. cases	Mean	S.D.	No. cases	Mean	S.D.
Group I—First test	18	114.5	12.0	20	117.5	17.3	18	116.2	13.4	56	116.1	14.6
Second test	18	118.9	16.7	20	128.5	21.3	18	127.8	12.0	56	125.0	18.4
Group II—First test	10	107.5	14.2	7	113.1	16.4	12	114.5	12.2	29	111.7	14.4
Second test	10	114.5	28.3	7	118.8	22.6	12	124.5	11.5	29	119.7	15.0
Group III—First test	42	107.1	11.4	38	105.0	17.5	49	110.2	13.6	129	107.7	14.4
Second test	42	111.2	13.6	38	110.8	18.1	49	117.4	13.6	129	113.4	15.4
Group IV—First test	24	102.0	11.6	27	106.7	16.2	28	106.6	17.6	79	105.3	15.7
Second test	24	104.1	15.1	27	106.7	18.7	28	112.7	16.3	79	108.0	17.2
Group V—First test	18	106.2	13.8	17	101.0	18.5	13	106.8	18.0	48	104.3	17.3
Second test	18	106.2	16.1	17	103.3	22.5	13	114.5	15.7	48	107.4	19.0
Group VI—First test	10	95.5	10.4	17	91.6	15.2	12	102.8	15.2	39	96.0	14.9
Second test	10	89.5	9.2	17	90.4	17.8	12	108.7	11.2	39	95.8	16.5
Totals—First test	122	106.1	13.2	126	105.5	18.5	132	109.7	15.5	380	107.1	16.0
Second test	122	108.7	16.0	126	109.3	22.6	132	117.4	15.0	380	111.9	18.6

obtained has been presented, not because of any intrinsic value which it possesses, but in the hope that it may serve as a stimulus to further work in this field.

Paternal occupation and intelligence of offspring.—Since paternal occupation was the chief criterion used in selecting cases for the main experimental group, it is interesting to note the relationship between this factor and IQ. Table 12 summarizes the data for all cases who were given two or more satisfactory tests.

The reports of the army intelligence tests show a decided relationship between score earned on the tests and occupational class. A similar relationship has been found between the intelligence test scores earned by school children and the occupational status of their parents.[3] These data show that similar intellectual differences between social classes are to be found among children of from two to four years of age. The difference between the mean IQ earned on the first examination by the children of parents belonging to the professional classes, and the corresponding rating for the children of day laborers amounts to approximately one and one-fourth standard deviations of the total distribution of IQs for the entire group. Considering the three age groups separately, the difference is 1.5 standard deviations at age two; 1.4 standard deviations at age three; and 0.8 standard deviations at age four. Since the number of cases at each age is small, the apparent decrease in the difference between the groups with increasing age is probably due to chance, but it is interesting to note that it appears to be at least as well established at the age of two as with the older children. Taken as a whole,

[3] M. E. Haggerty and H. B. Nash, "Mental Capacity of Children and Paternal Occupation," *J. of Educ. Psychol.*, Vol. 15 (1924), pp. 559-72.

Hector McDonald, "The Social Distribution of Intelligence in the Isle of Wight," *Brit. J. of Psychol.*, Vol. 16 (1925), pp. 123-29.

L. M. Terman et al., *Genetic Studies of Genius*, Vol. 1, pp. 61-72.

the findings show a most striking agreement with those reported by Haggerty in the article cited, which is based upon the examination of 6,688 New York State school children in grades 3-8 inclusive. A study of Haggerty's data shows that the difference between the median IQ of the 349 children from the professional classes and the 745 children of unskilled laborers is 1.4 standard deviations of the total distribution of the IQs in his group.[4] It appears from our data that, however intellectual differences between social classes may originate, they have at least become well established before the age of two years, while the close correspondence between the numerical results of the two studies affords strong presumptive evidence that the trait measured is one which is likely to be affected little or not at all by later training. The significance of this finding can hardly be overestimated.

TABLE 13

MEANS AND STANDARD DEVIATIONS OF IQ RATINGS BY SOURCE OF SUPPLY
(Total group, excluding cases of poor cooperation)

	Test 1			Test 2		
	Cases	Mean	S.D.	Cases	Mean	S.D.
By voluntary application	131	112.9	14.3	110	121.2	15.9
By home visit and invitation	76	110.7	17.0	62	117.4	18.9
Infant Welfare Clinics	116	106.4	13.2	87	109.3	15.0
Day Nurseries	94	102.6	16.8	75	105.4	18.0
Family Welfare Association	9	96.7	12.3	9	100.4	18.5
Children's Protective Society	39	98.9	14.6	29	97.8	12.5
Orphanage	10	86.5	8.7	8	87.0	6.6
Total	475	106.9	16.0	380	111.9	18.6

If we compare the ratings made by the different groups on the second test, the differences are even more striking, owing

[4] Haggerty reports only the median IQ for the separate groups. Since the distributions appear to be nearly symmetrical, the use of this figure with the standard deviation in place of the mean is not likely to have introduced any appreciable error.

FIGURE V

CHANGES IN IQ FROM FIRST TO SECOND TEST ACCORDING TO PATERNAL
OCCUPATION (Expressed in tenths of standard deviation from the
mean of each distribution).

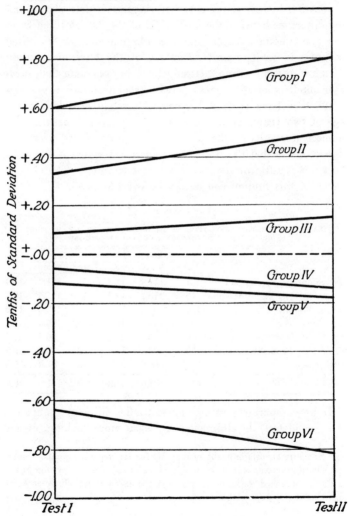

to the fact that the children of the upper occupational classes tend to make a greater gain in IQ from test to test than do those in the lower groups. This interesting and curious point will be taken up in some detail later on. The extent of the tendency is shown graphically in Figure V.

It was shown in Figure II that paternal occupation and source of supply are closely interrelated. It is not, therefore, surprising to find differences in the mean intelligence level of children obtained from various sources. The extent of these differences is shown in Table 13. The question then arises, whether these latter differences are purely functions of the different distributions of occupational classes within the supply groups, or whether the source of supply in itself has acted as a further selective factor through a tendency to include one or another of the intellectual extremes rather than representative members of the various occupational groups. In order to test the latter hypothesis, a distribution was made of the IQs of children of occupational groups III and IV from each of the several sources of supply, and the means and variabilities computed. The results are shown in Table 14. A comparison of these data with those presented in Tables 12 and 13, shows that some further selection of the kind indicated has been operative. It appears, however, to have affected the selection about equally in both directions, and for this reason it is probable that the norms for the total group have not been greatly disturbed thereby.

Selective elimination.—Figures III and IV show the number of cases from each of the various occupational groups and sources of supply who were eliminated from the main experimental group, together with reasons for elimination. Since the means and standard deviations of IQs earned on the first test by the eliminated cases are about identical with those of the main experimental group, there is no reason for believing that elimination has affected the results to an appreciable

TABLE 14

COMPARISON OF IQ RATINGS EARNED ON THE FIRST TEST BY CHILDREN OF
OCCUPATIONAL GROUPS III AND IV FROM DIFFERENT SOURCES OF SUPPLY

	By voluntary application	By home visit and invitation	Infant Welfare Clinics	Day Nurseries	Family Welfare Association	Children's Protective Society	Orphanage
Cases	66	31	85	47	7	17	3
Mean IQ	113.0	107.7	106.5	105.1	98.8	101.0	81.2
S.D.	13.5	14.9	12.9	15.6	12.9	14.1	4.7

degree. Table 15, which gives means and standard deviations
of the IQ ratings for each of the three main groups, shows
clearly that this is not a chance result, but has been brought
about by maintaining a balance between eliminative factors
not under control (cases not retested) and those under control (retested cases not included in the main experimental
group) through the use of a standard criterion such as is afforded by the distribution of paternal occupations. The greatest amount of uncontrollable elimination has come from the
middle and lower occupational levels, while the controlled
elimination has come chiefly from the upper occupational
classes.

RELIABILITY OF THE SCALE AS A WHOLE

Changes in IQ from first to second test.—Figure VI shows
the distribution of changes in IQ from the first to the second
test for the total retest group according to examiners. The
mean algebraic change for this group was 4.9 points of IQ.
This is slightly greater than was found for the main experimental group, for whom the corresponding figure was 4.4
points. The mean arithmetical change (disregarding sign)
for this group was 8.6 points; for the main experimental
group, 8.5 points. It has been mentioned before that the
tendency toward increase in IQ on the second test was found

TABLE 15

MEANS AND STANDARD DEVIATIONS OF IQs EARNED ON THE FIRST TEST BY GROUP CLASSIFICATION

Group	Age 2			Age 8			Age 4			Total		
	N	Mean	S.D.	N	Mean	S.D.	N	Mean	S.D.	N	Mean	S.D.
Main Experimental Group	100	105.1	13.0	100	104.4	18.2	100	109.4	16.6	300	106.3	16.2
Retested cases not included in main experimental group*	22	111.8	18.1	26	115.3	24.5	32	121.4	13.1	80	116.8	19.2
Cases not retested*	36	107.6	13.1	33	103.6	16.8	26	106.8	17.2	95	106.0	15.7

*Exclusive of cases of poor cooperation.

to be greatest for the four-year-olds and least for the two-year-olds. The age differences in the arithmetical change are in the same direction but are very slight in amount.

Figure VI shows no significant differences associated with change of examiner. The one apparent exception is found in those cases in which the first test was given by Examiner B, the second by Examiner A, where the tendency toward an increase of IQ on the second test is somewhat less than was found for the other groups. If this difference were due either to more lenient standards on the part of one of the examiners, or to differences in their respective ability to secure a maximum response from the children, a compensating tendency in the opposite direction would be seen when the order of

FIGURE VI

CHANGES IN IQ FROM FIRST TO SECOND TEST ACCORDING TO EXAMINERS.

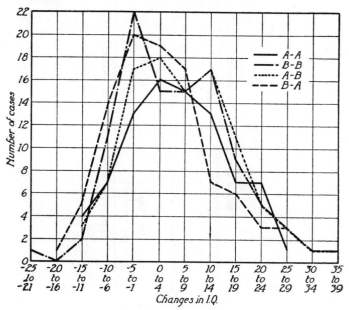

examiners was reversed. This tendency is not apparent. The true explanation seems to lie in the fact that this group of cases includes a disproportionate number of children who belong to the lower occupational groups. Table 12 and Figure V show that the gain in IQ rating from first to second test is ordinarily much less for these children than for those who come from the higher occupational groups.

In an attempt to ascertain the basis for this apparent differential rate of gain, a number of hypotheses were tested. A possible explanation is that the more intelligent children may tend to profit by the first experience to a greater extent than do those of less ability. This would be in accordance with the results of certain laboratory experiments in learning, which have shown that in tasks involving the higher mental processes, equalization of practice tends to increase, rather than decrease, the differences originally found among the members of a group.[5] In order to test this hypothesis the correlations between initial IQ and gain or loss from first to second test were computed for each of the three age groups separately, and the raw correlations thus obtained were corrected for regression by the use of the Thomson formula.[6]

[5] G. M. Ruch, "The Influence of the Factor of Intelligence on the Form of the Learning Curve," *Psychol. Mon.*, Vol. 35 (1925), No. 160.

[6] G. H. Thomson, "A Formula to Correct for the Effect of Errors of Measurement on the Correlation of Initial Values with Gains," *J. of Exper. Psychol.*, Vol. 7 (1925), pp. 321-24.

$$r_{ag} = \frac{r_{xy} + \dfrac{S.D._x}{S.D._y}(1 - r_x)}{\dfrac{1}{S.D._y}\sqrt{r_x(S.D._y^2 - S.D._x^2(1 - r_x)) - S.D._z^2(1 - r_z)}}$$

Where x = measured initial value

y = measured gain

z = measured final value

and r_x and r_z are reliability coefficients

The results, which are given in Table 16, show that when correction is made for the unreliability of the scale, a positive correlation between initial IQ and gain is found to exist, although this tendency does not appear in the uncorrected values.

TABLE 16

CORRELATION BETWEEN INITIAL IQ AND CHANGE IN IQ FROM FIRST TO
SECOND TEST
(Total Retest Group)

Uncorrected	Age 2	Age 3	Age 4
r	—.014	+.078	—.055
P.E.	.084	.083	.082
Corrected*			
r	+.277	+.356	+.503
P.E.	.079	.074	.064

*By use of Thomson formula.

A second possible explanation is to be found in the assumption that the children of the upper occupational groups have been unduly influenced by special training or coaching on the test elements during the interval between tests. Such training might, of course, be unintentional, amounting to little more than persistent attempt on the part of the parent who had some general acquaintance with the tests to satisfy herself as to the child's actual ability. It is obviously impossible to ascertain with precision the extent to which such training has taken place, but it seems reasonable to suppose that it would be more likely to occur in those cases where the parent was actually present during the examination and thus had had an opportunity not only to become acquainted with the nature of the test elements but to observe specific instances of success and failure on the part of the child. In nearly all cases the presence or absence of the mother was recorded in the general observational notes made at the time of the examination. In a few instances this fact was not recorded. Since the presence of the mother was the exception rather than the rule, it is highly probable that failure to record ordinarily indicates that the mother was not present. However, for the sake of complete accuracy, such cases have been treated separately. The relationship of presence of mother to gain or loss in IQ is shown in Table 17. It should be noted that cases in which the door between the examining room and the room in which the mother was seated was left open have been included among those cases in which the mother actually remained in the room, since this arrangement frequently made it possible for her to overhear the responses.

The children whose mothers were present at the time of the first examination show no significantly greater tendency toward increase of rating on the second examination than do those whose mothers were not present. It seems unlikely, therefore, that specific coaching has had any appreciable effect upon the results.

An additional factor to be considered is the comparative accuracy of the two tests. It is obvious that existent differences between groups will only be made apparent by means of a suitable measuring instrument, and that in so far as the results of the measurement are affected by chance, or by other factors unrelated to the general field of inquiry, both the means and standard deviations of the various sub groups will approach more closely to the general mean and standard deviation derived from the total distribution. If, therefore, factors which are unrelated to either variable enter into the results of one test more than the other, it is to be expected that, all other conditions being equal, that test which is less affected by adventitious factors will show the clearest separation between groups actually differing with regard to the trait in question. This is, of course, simply another way of saying that the correlation between two variables as obtained through the use of fallible measuring instruments can never, except by chance,

TABLE 17

MEANS AND STANDARD DEVIATIONS OF CHANGES IN IQ ACCORDING TO PRESENCE OR ABSENCE OF MOTHER

	Age 2			Age 3			Age 4			Total		
	No. cases	Mean	S.D.	No. cases	Mean	S.D.	No. cases	Mean	S.D.	No. cases	Mean	S.D.
Mother present	51	2.3	9.6	19	6.0	7.4	4	4.5	9.0	74	3.4	9.2
Mother not present	62	1.5	10.3	104	4.5	11.4	124	7.4	9.3	290	5.1	10.6
Not recorded	9	5.3	8.7	3	7.0	14.7	4	12.0	0.8	16	7.3	9.5
Total	122	2.1	9.9	126	4.8	11.0	132	7.5	9.2	380	4.9	10.3

TABLE 18

CORRELATIONS BETWEEN FIRST AND SECOND TEST BY AGE AND SEX
(Main Experimental Group)

	Age 2			Age 3			Age 4			Total		
	Boys	Girls	Total	Boys	Girls	Total	Boys	Girls	Total	Boys	Girls	Total
r	.810	.705	.759	.817	.902	.869	.832	.809	.821	.820	.806	.813
P.E.	.032	.049	.029	.031	.018	.015	.028	.032	.020	.015	.020	.012

56

be greater than that obtained through true measurement, and will ordinarily be appreciably lower. If an improvement in the measuring instrument used for one variable is brought about, either by an increase in reliability or in validity (with reference to the particular trait considered), the other variable remaining as before, an increase in the obtained correlation is to be expected. This increase in correlation involves a change in the slope of the regression line with a consequent increase in the absolute difference between the means of the positive and negative arrays. That such a difference in the favor of the second of the two tests probably does exist in the case under consideration is indicated by three distinct sources of evidence: (a) the correlation between the ratings obtained for the first and second tests as compared to those on the second and third for 56 cases who were given a third test after an appreciably longer interval; (b) correlation between half-scales on each of the two tests corrected by the Spearman-Brown formula; and (c) the internal consistency of the separate items with the total, calculated by the method of biserial r. It will be shown that the second and third of these criteria show a distinct difference in favor of the second test, while the first shows no significant difference between the two in spite of the longer interval.

TABLE 19

RELIABILITY OF TOTAL SCALE AS DETERMINED BY THE CORRELATION BETWEEN HALF-SCALES USING THE SPEARMAN-BROWN FORMULA
(Main Experimental Group)

	Age 2			Age 3			Age 4		
	Boys	Girls	Total	Boys	Girls	Total	Boys	Girls	Total
First test									
r	.853	.836	.845	.899	.913	.910	.816	.865	.854
P.E.	.026	.027	.020	.018	.017	.012	.029	.024	.019
Second test									
r	.886	.929	.911	.921	.921	.921	.861	.892	.883
P.E.	.020	.016	.012	.016	.016	.011	.025	.019	.014

Reliability coefficients.—Table 18 shows by ages and sexes separately the correlation between the IQs earned on the first and second tests for the 300 cases of the main experimental group. Table 19 shows the reliability of the total, as calculated by the correlation between half-scales when corrected by the use of the Spearman-Brown formula.

Neither of these methods is wholly satisfactory. The first method may be criticized on the grounds that (a) it necessitates a correlation between indices rather than between absolute measures in order to allow for differences in rate of growth, since at these early ages, such differences introduce significant changes in the IQ even during the short interval considered; (b) practice effect is not excluded; (c) apart from practice effect in the ordinary sense of the term, some children may profit by the first experience to the extent of questioning other children or adults with regard to certain points in the scale and thus increase their ratings on the second test; (d) true fluctuations in rate of mental development may occur during the interval between tests, hence lack of correspondence of the two ratings is not necessarily an indication of lack of precision in the measuring instrument.

The second method, which is based upon the correlation between half-scales corrected by means of the Spearman-Brown formula, is equally open to objection though for different reasons. Since no interval is involved, the correlation may be calculated between the absolute number of tests passed in each half-scale, and thus the error due to the use of indices may be avoided; neither is there any real question of practice effect. For complete validity, however, the formula requires that the intercorrelations and standard deviations of the unitary tests must be equal.[7] When only a single pair of unitary tests

[7] See G. M. Ruch, Luton Ackerson, and Jesse D. Jackson, "An Empirical Study of the Spearman-Brown Formula as applied to Educational Test Material," *J. of Educ. Psychol.*, Vol. 17 (1926), pp. 309-313.

is employed, however, as in the present instance of correlation between half-scales, it is customary to consider that the conditions are sufficiently fulfilled for a single approximation if the two half-scales are closely similar.[8]

A source of error in the application of this formula which may be of considerable importance, especially when the treatment of data derived from young children is concerned, lies in the fact that elements which are incident to the immediate situation but are unrelated to the general field may bring about a spurious increase in the magnitude of the coefficient obtained. For example, such factors as shyness, irritability due to temporary indisposition, etc. may affect the complete situation to a marked degree on one occasion and little or not at all on another occasion. It is quite true that in the final analysis this is a question of the validity rather than of the reliability of the measuring instrument; but it is also true that the use of this method may introduce the rather confusing result of bringing about an apparent increase in reliability through the operation of factors which decrease validity. When adequate criteria by which validity may be determined are available, the matter becomes of less importance, since it is then possible to check up the question of spurious reliability[9] arising through the introduction of factors unrelated to the trait under consideration. Since no entirely adequate criteria for the results of the mental examination of preschool-age children are at present available (except the rather inconvenient one of waiting for the children to reach an age at which tests whose validity has been established may be applied), the importance of careful investigation of the apparent effect

[8] T. L. Kelley, *Statistical Method.* (New York: Macmillan Co., 1923). See pages 205-207.

[9] "Spurious" of course only in the sense of being unrelated to the field of measurement.

upon the test results of factors such as have been mentioned can hardly be overestimated.

For the reasons which have just been discussed, the data presented in Tables 18 and 19 should not be regarded as more than approximations to the true value of the reliability coefficient. Nevertheless, a comparison of the different values obtained shows certain extremely significant tendencies. The correlation between half-scales is higher for the second test than for the first at all ages and for both sexes. While the difference is not great, the consistency with which it is maintained leaves little room for doubt that a true difference in reliability exists, since whatever doubt may be expressed as to the complete suitability of the method, a comparison of the two results is presumably entirely valid, inasmuch as the objections which may be put forth apply equally in the two instances.

An almost equally consistent difference is seen when the reliability computed on the basis of the correlation between retests (Table 18) is compared with that derived by the half-scale method. With the single exception of the four-year-old boys, these coefficients are all lower than those calculated on either of the two tests by the half-scale method. This is quite contrary to the usual expectation. It has been said that under usual conditions the correlation between retests may be safely considered to constitute an upper limit for the reliability coefficient, while that derived by the Spearman-Brown formula from somewhat dissimilar halves of a test would constitute a lower limit.[10] The fact that in this instance the relationship between the results obtained by the two methods has been reversed makes it extremely likely that some factor or factors not usually considered have entered into the situation. Kelley's

[10] T. L. Kelley, *Statistical Method*. See pages 203-204.

comment on the general desirability of a fore-exercise may well be considered here. (See reference just cited.)

SUMMARY

1. The Kuhlman 1922 Revision of the Binet Scale was given to three groups of Minneapolis children aged two, three, and four years respectively. One hundred cases were included in each group. These children were selected to constitute a representative sampling of the population of the city, on the basis of a comparison between the distribution of paternal occupations with those reported by the 1920 census. Besides the 300 children selected on this basis, 195 additional children within the same age range were given at least one examination, making a total of 495 cases available for study.

2. Each of the 300 selected cases was given a second test after an average interval of 5.9 weeks. The IQ ratings obtained on the second test were, in general, distinctly higher than those on the first. The mean algebraic difference between the two ratings was 3.0 points for the two-year-olds, 3.2 points for the three-year-olds, and 6.6 points for the four-year-olds. It is shown that this tendency to gain in rating is not distributed at random, but is greatest for the children whose fathers belong to the professional classes; while the children of day laborers not only make no consistent gain, but on the average show a slight tendency to rank lower on the second test than they did on the first. Possible reasons for this apparent discrepancy are discussed.

3. On both tests, the children whose fathers belong to the upper occupational groups average distinctly higher in intelligence rating than do those of the lower classes. While a similar relationship between paternal occupation and intelligence of offspring has previously been demonstrated in the case of

adults, and also for school children, it is now shown for the first time that individuals coming from the various social classes present equal, if not even more marked differences in intelligence as early as the age of two, three, or four years.

4. All tests were given by two examiners. In each age group, 25 of the tests were made by Examiner A on both occasions, 25 by Examiner B on both occasions, 25 first by Examiner A, then by Examiner B, and 25 first by Examiner B, then by Examiner A. Comparison of the results failed to reveal any significant differences which could be attributed to a change of examiners.

5. The children were obtained from seven different sources of supply, each of which is described. A high correlation was found to exist between source of supply and paternal occupation, but apart from its relationship to paternal occupation, the source of supply operates as a further selective factor in determining the average intellectual level of the children obtained through its agency. The bearing of this fact upon the representative character of the group under consideration is discussed.

6. Data concerning other possible selective factors, such as uncontrollable elimination and racial stock, are presented and discussed.

7. The reliability of the scale as a whole is considered in relationship to three possible methods of determination: (a) changes in IQ from first to second test, (b) correlation between first and second test, and (c) correlation between half-scales corrected by the Spearman-Brown formula. It is shown that the mean algebraic change in IQ from first to second test averages 4.4 points and is greatest for the four-year-olds and least for the two-year-olds. The absolute change, disregarding sign, averages 8.5 points. The differences between the three age-groups in respect to absolute change are in the

same direction but much less in amount than was found true with regard to the algebraic change. The correlation between IQs earned on the first and second test for the total group of 300 cases was .820± .015. The reliability as determined by the correlation between half-scales, using the Spearman-Brown formula, averaged .870 for the first test and .905 for the second test. Possible reasons for the discrepancy in the findings by the two methods are discussed.

CHAPTER IV

ANALYSIS OF RESULTS: THE SEPARATE TESTS IN THE SCALE

Since the reliability of a whole is obviously a function of the reliability of the separate parts of which it is composed, and since few of the tests in the Binet series have been studied specifically with view to determining their reliability, the findings to be presented in this chapter should be of especial interest to research workers who are interested in test construction. The following summarized statement indicates the amount of data upon which results have been based.

The usual rule for complete testing, which requires the establishment of a basal year at which all tests are passed and continuation of testing until a year group has been reached at which all tests are failed, was adhered to throughout, with the exception of certain instances in which failure on a given test was assumed on the basis of previous failure on an easier test of the same type. These exceptions were specifically noted and described at the end of Chaper II. In the course of the two examinations, the two-year series of tests was given 611 times; the three-year series, 774 times; the four-year series, 809 times; the five-year series, 624 times; the six-year series, 376 times; the seven-year series, 333 times; and the eight-year series, 172 times. These numbers are greatly in excess of those reported by Kuhlman for the original standardization. (See page 12 of the manual previously cited.)

The data have been treated with reference to the following points: (1) the placement of the tests in year groups, (2) their reliability as indicated by changes in success from first to second examination, (3) internal consistency of the scale, as indicated by the correlation of each of the separate tests with the remainder of the scale, and (4) the motivating power of the various tests, as indicated by the apparent interest shown by the children while taking them.

TABLE 20

Test Numbers	Age 2			Age 3			Age 4		
	Boys	Girls	Total	Boys	Girls	Total	Boys	Girls	Total
Below 18 months				No failures recorded at any age level.					
18 Mo. Series									
Test 1	94	100	97	100	100	100	100	100	100
2	92	96	94	98	100	99	100	100	100
3	90	98	94	98	100	99	100	100	100
4	98	100	99	100	100	100	100	100	100
5	94	98	96	100	100	100	100	100	100
2 Yr. Series									
Test 1	58	62	60	98	96	97	100	100	100
2	58	46	52	96	96	96	100	100	100
3	90	86	88	98	100	99	100	100	100
4	46	40	43	92	94	93	100	100	100
5	96	96	96	100	100	100	100	100	100
3 Yr. Series									
Test 1	14	22	18	76	80	78	96	98	97
2	64	72	68	98	98	98	100	100	100
3	10	8	9	42	62	52	84	92	88
4	10	8	9	52	70	61	92	100	96
5	42	48	45	88	92	90	100	100	100
6	30	20	25	82	88	85	100	100	100
7	0	0	0	24	30	27	80	86	83
8	0	0	0	12	22	17	80	84	82
4 Yr. Series									
Test 1	12	6	9	54	54	54	86	92	89
2	10	6	8	48	70	59	92	96	94
3	20	8	14	60	60	60	92	92	92
4	0	0	0	8	24	16	70	76	73
5	2	0	1	8	8	8	58	74	66
6	0	0	0	6	8	7	36	56	46
7	0	2	1	34	42	38	82	88	85
8	0	0	0	6	12	9	40	56	48

TABLE 20 (*Continued*)

Test Numbers	Age 2			Age 3			Age 4		
	Boys	Girls	Total	Boys	Girls	Total	Boys	Girls	Total
5 Yr. Series									
Test 1	..	..	..	0	8	4	26	26	26
2	..	..	..	2	0	1	6	10	8
3	..	..	..	10	10	10	42	58	50
4	..	.	..	4	6	5	22	38	30
5	..	..	..	14	8	11	38	62	50
6	..	..	..	6	18	12	42	48	45
7	..	..	..	2	4	3	38	44	41
8	..	..	..	0	6	3	18	20	19
6 Yr. Series									
Test 1	..	..	..	8	4	6	24	22	23
•2	..	..	..	10	20	15	34	62	48
3	..	..	..	6	14	10	34	44	39
4	..	..	..	0	4	2	26	46	36
5	..	..	..	6	12	9	44	58	51
6	..	..	..	0	0	0	4	4	4
7	..	..	..	2	0	1	8	20	14
8	..	..	..	0	0	0	10	20	15
7 Yr. Series									
Test 1	..	..	..	0	2	1	18	28	23
2	..	..	..	0	2	1	4	12	8
3	..	..	..	0	0	0	0	0	0
4	..	..	..	0	4	2	16	24	20
5	..	..	..	0	0	0	4	2	3
6	..	..	..	0	0	0	2	0	1
7	..	..	..	0	0	0	0	0	0
8	..	..	..	0	0	0	0	0	0
8 Yr. Series									
Test 1	..	..	..	0	0	0	0	0	0
2	..	..	..	0	0	0	0	0	0
3	..	..	..	0	0	0	0	0	0
4	..	..	..	0	0	0	0	0	0
5	..	..	..	0	0	0	0	0	0
6	..	..	..	0	0	0	0	0	0
7	..	..	..	0	0	0	0	0	0
8	..	..	..	0	0	0	0	0	0
9 years or over.				No tests passed at any age level.					

Placement of the tests in year groups.—Table 20 shows the percentages succeeding with each of the separate tests in the scale at the time of the first examination, by ages and sexes separately. These figures are based upon the main experimental group.

On page 47 of the manual of directions, Kuhlman makes the following comment with regard to the importance of correct placement of the tests:

"Theoretically these percentages [of passes at a given age level] may vary from the ideally correct figure, provided that they do so in equal amounts above and below, so that the average for all the tests in the age-group will be correct for the groups. . . . . . The misplacement of a few tests does not affect the accuracy of the scale as seriously as it might seem, and if the misplacements are distributed in the right way, the accuracy may not be affected at all."

As far as group averages are concerned, this statement is perhaps true, but that misplacement of tests may seriously affect the accuracy of individual ratings can hardly be doubted. Suppose, for instance, that two tests, actually belonging at the four-year level, are placed in the three-year series and that this is compensated for by placing two other tests, actually belonging at the five-year level, in the six-year series. A child makes a basal year of two. He passes seven tests at the three-year level, five at the four-year level, but none at the five-year level. The six-year tests are accordingly not tried. Had they been given, it is quite possible that he might have passed one or both of the two misplaced tests. Moreover, had these tests been properly placed at the five-year level, the child would then have been given a chance at the remaining tests of the six-year series, and while it is improbable that he would have passed more than one or two of these at most, it is by no means certain that he would have failed on all. In other words, even though a balance is maintained with regard to the direction of misplaced tests, individual errors may still result through incomplete testing consequent upon the apparent establishment of complete failure at too early an age-level. Errors in the opposite direction may be brought about in a similar fashion, through the establishment of a basal year at too high a point and consequent automatic assignment of credit for tests which, had they actually been given, might very probably have been failed. With children of school age, spurious gain or loss of credit on one or two tests affects the IQ but little; at these early ages the difference may be quite significant. At the age of three years, success or failure on a single test affects the total rating to the extent of a little over four points of IQ; while at the age of ten, a single test counts for only slightly more than one IQ point. Moreover, misplacement of tests tends to increase the apparent "scatter" and thereby lengthens the time required for testing without a corresponding improvement in accuracy. Correct placement of tests, especially at the early ages, is therefore a matter of importance.

Reliability of Separate Tests.—A rough estimate of the comparative reliability of the various tests in the scale may be obtained by comparing the frequency and direction of variation in success from first to second test. Table 21 summarizes these changes for the main experimental group. It should be noted that some degree of positive change, i.e., from failure on the first test to success on the second test, is to be expected as a result of normal growth during the six weeks interval. Negative changes, or changes from success on the first test to failure on the second test, theoretically should not occur. Exceptionally frequent positive changes are also presumably an indication of unreliability.

TABLE 21

POSITIVE AND NEGATIVE CHANGES IN PERFORMANCE ON THE VARIOUS SUBTESTS
(Main Experimental Group)

Note: By positive changes are meant cases in which children who failed on
a given test at the time of the first examination, passed it on the second.
Negative changes include cases in which a test that was passed on the first examination was failed on the second. Some degree of positive change is to be
anticipated as a result of normal growth during the six weeks interval; negative changes, theoretically, should not occur.

Test Numbers	Age 2 Positive	Age 2 Negative	Age 3 Positive	Age 3 Negative	Age 4 Positive	Age 4 Negative	Total Positive	Total Negative
2 Yr. Series								
Test 1	15	0	1	0	..	..	16	0
2	14	6	3	1	..	..	17	7
3	9	0	0	0	..	..	9	0
4	19	7	3	3	..	..	22	10
5	4	0	0	1	..	..	4	1
3 Yr. Series								
Test 1	14	5	10	1	3	0	27	6
2	17	2	0	0	0	0	17	2
3	9	2	8	7	7	2	24	11
4	10	1	19	11	4	1	33	13
5	17	1	5	3	1	0	23	4
6	14	3	10	3	0	0	24	6
7	1	0	15	1	11	1	27	2
8	1	0	20	1	14	0	35	1
4 Yr. Series								
Test 1	5	3	11	5	10	2	26	10
2	12	0	16	11	6	5	34	16
3	10	9	16	12	6	4	32	25
4	0	0	12	3	13	2	25	5
5	0	1	9	0	21	2	30	3
6	0	0	16	1	25	3	41	4
7	2	0	14	5	10	7	26	12
8	0	0	9	1	25	6	34	7
5 Yr. Series								
Test 1	..	..	1	4	5	9	6	13
2	..	..	1	1	6	2	7	3
3	..	..	11	3	25	5	36	8

TABLE 21 (*Continued*)

Test Numbers	Age 2 Posi-tive	Age 2 Nega-tive	Age 3 Posi-tive	Age 3 Nega-tive	Age 4 Posi-tive	Age 4 Nega-tive	Total Posi-tive	Total Nega-tive
4	..	..	7	2	16	9	23	11
5	..	..	5	3	20	3	25	6
6	..	..	5	4	25	5	30	9
7	..	..	7	1	25	6	32	7
8	..	..	6	2	9	2	15	4
6 Yr. Series								
Test 1	..	..	3	4	18	11	21	15
2	..	..	8	2	23	6	31	8
3	..	..	12	4	19	16	31	20
4	..	..	5	0	18	4	23	4
5	..	..	13	2	21	6	34	8
6	..	..	1	0	6	3	7	3
7	..	..	1	0	6	6	7	6
8	..	..	2	0	11	4	13	4
7 Yr. Series								
Test 1	..	..	5	1	18	8	23	9
2	..	..	1	1	4	3	5	4
3	..	..	0	0	0	0	0	0
4	..	..	8	1	20	3	28	4
5	..	..	0	0	3	2	3	2
6	..	..	0	0	4	1	4	1
7	..	..	0	0	0	0	0	0
8	..	..	0	0	0	0	0	0
8 Yr. Series								
Test 1	..	..	..	..	0	0	0	0
2	..	..	..	..	0	0	0	0
3	..	..	..	..	0	0	0	0
4	..	..	..	..	0	0	0	0
5	..	..	..	..	1	0	1	0
6	..	..	..	..	1	0	1	0
7	..	..	..	..	0	0	0	0
8	..	..	..	..	0	0	0	0

Change in success from test to test was also tabulated with reference to change in examiner. No statistically reliable differences were found, but there were a few instances in which the possibility of a difference in reliability associated with change of examiner was indicated. These cases will be taken up in connection with discussion of the individual tests at the end of this chapter.

Internal consistency of the scale, as measured by the correlation of the individual tests with the mental-age score earned on the remainder of the scale, excluding the test under consideration.—Table 22 shows the correlation of each of the individual tests with the remainder of the scale computed by the method of biserial r. In interpreting these data it must be remembered that low correlation of an individual test with the remaining total score is not necessarily an indication that the test is either unreliable or invalid. A test which has few elements in common with the remainder of the scale, but which shows a high correlation with the criterion, is, for that very reason, more valuable than another which merely duplicates other items in the scale. However, in the absence of adequate criteria by which validity may be judged, a test which shows exceptionally low correlation with the total is ordinarily to be regarded with some suspicion, especially if the reliability as shown by retest is also low.

It is possible that these correlations have in some instances been spuriously increased by the practice of assigning automatic credit for all tests below the basal year and assuming failure in all later tests after a year-group has been reached at which all tests were failed. However, the amount of such error is probably small. It is most likely to have occurred in the case of tests of low reliability, such as Vl 1, and VI 3, where the obtained correlation with mental age may be quite largely due to the fact that the more backward children had

TABLE 22

INTERNAL CONSISTENCY:

BISERIAL CORRELATION OF EACH OF THE SEPARATE SUBTESTS IN THE SCALE WITH MENTAL AGE SCORE ON REMAINDER OF THE SCALE

(Main Experimental Group)

Test Numbers	Age 2		Age 3		Age 4	
	Test 1	Test 2	Test 1	Test 2	Test 1	Test 2
2 Yr. Series						
Test 1	.895	.853	......	......	......	......
2	.660	.825	......	......	......	......
3	.456	......	......	......	......	......
4	.736	.576	......	......	......	......
5	......	......	......	......	......	......
3 Yr. Series						
Test 1	.469	.577	.716	.661	......	......
2	.684	.787	......	......	......	......
3	......	......	.752	.823	.540	......
4	......	......	.696	.686	......	......
5	.734	.830	......	......	......	......
6	.780	.879	.715	......	......	......
7	......	......	.879	.829	.520	......
8	......	......	.764	.944	.428	......
4 Yr. Series						
Test 1	......	......	.712	.740	.415	......
2	......	......	.661	.675	......	......
3	.694	.415	.656	.674	......	......
4	......	......	.932	.945	.562	.746
5	......	......	......	......	.563	.595
6	......	......	......	......	.635	.683
7	......	......	.691	.797	.550	.543
8	......	......	......	......	.619	.584
5 Yr. Series						
Test 1	......	......	......	......	.614	.722
2	......	......	......	......	......	......
3	......	......	.731	.858	.547	.609
4	......	......	......	......	.514	.619
5	......	......	.662	.797	.606	.568
6	......	......	.830	.902	.561	.560
7	......	......	......	......	.622	.511
8	......	......	......	......	.511	.264

TABLE 22 (*Continued*)

Test Numbers	Age 2		Age 3		Age 4	
	Test 1	Test 2	Test 1	Test 2	Test 1	Test 2
6 Yr. Series						
Test 1	......	......	......	......	.355	.261
2	......	......	.893	.922	.512	.594
3	......	......	.766	.900	.285	.436
4	......	......	......	......	.676	.448
5	......	......	......	......	.562	.666
6	......	......	......	......	......	......
7	......	......	......	......	.591	.657
8	......	......	......	......	.642	.666
7 Yr. Series						
Test 1	......	......	......	......	.353	.398
4	......	......	......	......	.562	.649

Note: Correlations have been computed for dichotomies within the range of 10-90 per cent.

dropped out at a lower level, hence were not given these tests. The generally high correlations obtained for the three-year-old group are due to the high variability of the mental-age distributions for that group, a fact which has been mentioned before. (See Tables 6-7.)

Since only 100 cases are included in each group, correlations based upon extreme dichotomies would have little or no significance. We have, therefore, computed the correlations only for those age-groups in which the proportion of success on the test in question was within the range of 10-90 per cent.

Attractiveness.—An additional factor which must not be overlooked in any consideration of test material is the intrinsic interest of the task for children of the ages at which it is to be used. Tests which become attractive only by virtue of the artificial interest which can be aroused by a skillful examiner are uncertain instruments at best, and are entirely unsuited to the examination of little children who have not yet reached an age at which their own performance as such has any particular interest for them, and whose cooperation must, therefore, be secured through direct interest in the test itself. While it is true that an examiner who is experienced in handling children can, as a rule, stimulate some degree of interest in an otherwise uninteresting task, it is unwise to rely exclusively upon so variable a factor as this is likely to be.

In order to obtain some roughly quantitative data on the relative attractiveness of the separate tests for children at these early ages, the examiners made a practice of indicating, by means of a special symbol, those tests which the child seemed particularly to enjoy, while tests in which interest could be aroused only with considerable difficulty or which seemed to provoke antagonism were marked with a different symbol. These records were in all cases made at the time of testing. Children were not questioned as to their preferences, the judgment was made purely upon the basis of their spontaneous behavior. Tests were marked as "especially enjoyed" in those cases where the child's response was accompanied by laughter, by requests to "do it again," or by more than ordinary absorption of attention. Spontaneous comments such as "That's fun," "I like to do that," etc., were also frequently made. Tests marked as "disliked" were those which the child at first refused to attempt or of which he tired almost immediately after they had been begun, or those which were commented upon in such ways as "Aw, that's no good," "Don't let's do that any more," and the like. Only rather outstanding manifestations of preference or distaste were recorded. While the data obtained in this way are obviously extremely crude, they serve, nevertheless, to throw some light upon the highly important factor of motivation in test performance.

In the two-year series, tests 4, 3, 5, and 1 are "liked" more frequently than they are "disliked," and in the order mentioned. Test 2 is "disliked" four times as frequently as it is "liked."

Of the three-year series, tests 8, 7, 1, 5, and 2 are most frequently "liked," while tests 6, 4, and 3 are most "disliked."

In the four-year series, the most-liked tests are 4, 8, 5, 6, and 3. Test 2 is most frequently disliked, while tests 1 and 7 are rather neutral as regards attractiveness.

Test 8 is best liked of the five-year series. Test 5 is most often disliked and test 7 is best described as bi-modal, since some children evince strong antagonism toward it, while others find it particularly interesting. Tests 1, 2, 3, 4, and 6 are of rather neutral interest.

The order of interest value for the six-year tests is 5, 4, 2, and 7. Test 8, which is a more difficult form of the same type as test V 7, also has a rather bi-modal distribution of interest ratings, and tests 1, 3, and 6 are of neutral interest.

In the seven-year series, test 1 is most frequently liked, and test 4 is most disliked. The remaining tests show neutral interest value for our group.

It should be mentioned that tests which are either much too easy or much too difficult are usually quite neutral in their interest value for young children. Tests which are too easy are likely to be performed in a rather hasty, perfunctory fashion, while those which are entirely beyond the child's comprehension, although they seldom arouse interest, are also far less likely to bring forth negativistic reactions than is the case when the child understands what is required from him but does not want to do it. For example, we have not infrequently found children of two and three who show considerable ill temper over the three-year test of repeating sentences, but who, if the five-year series has to be given, respond merely with a rather vague stare or an uncertain "What?" which is in marked contrast to the vigorous "I won't" brought forth by the simpler situation of the same kind. The comparative infrequency of pronounced affective reactions to the tests at the upper age-levels is to be attributed to the youth of the subjects rather than to the nature of the tasks.

SUMMARY OF RESULTS ON THE INDIVIDUAL TESTS

Eighteen-months series.—Our data are inadequate to enable us to evaluate the tests at this age-level since so large a proportion of our subjects earned a basal year of two years or over, that the eighteen-months tests were not given. On *a priori* grounds, it seems somewhat unfortunate that three out of the five tests in the age group have to do with the child's eating habits, especially in view of the fact that training probably plays a large part in determining the exact age at which a child learns to drink from a cup or to use a spoon. These tests are, moreover, inconvenient to give in the laboratory, and test 4 (spitting out distasteful solids) is likely to arouse an emotional state which may carry over to other tests. We have credited these three tests on the basis of parents' reports, a procedure which is always open to question, since maternal fondness may often lead to an overestimation of the child's actual proficiency.

Test 3 (Use or understanding of speech) can usually be scored on the basis of incidental observation, a fact which is of distinct advantage with children at this age. Practically all of our two-year-olds pass this test.

Test 5 (Recognition of objects in pictures) is difficult to score consistently. On several occasions when both examiners were present during the giving of the test, they have been unable to agree as to the scoring. The directions for scoring read, "Passed if the child shows marked signs of recognition or interest by gaze or vocalization." Just how marked these signs must be, how long-continued the gaze, or what the nature of the vocalization, is difficult to say. Some of our eighteen-months-old children gaze intently at practically any object presented, others of apparently equal or more advanced development may be unable or unwilling to focus the attention upon any one thing for more than a few seconds. Nearly all our cases gave some degree of attention to the pictures as shown, but the significance of this was frequently uncertain. Unless a more objective scoring system can be devised, it appears questionable whether or not the test should be retained in the scale.

Two-year series.—Test 1 (Pointing out objects in pictures). This test ranks exceptionally high on all counts. It is unusually reliable, there being no instances of negative change from test to test, and the number of positive changes is probably not excessive, since in several instances these occurred after marginal failure at the time of the first test. Cases of marked interest in this test occur four-and-a-half times as frequently as those of active dislike for it. As a matter of fact, manifestations of dislike for this test are almost entirely confined to very young or backward children who completely fail to comprehend what is wanted. The biserial coefficient of correlation with the total mental age is above .85 for each of the two examinations. The test is correctly located at the two-year level.

Test 2 (Imitation of movements). This test is decidedly less reliable than the preceding one. There are 6 instances of negative and 14 of positive changes recorded for the 100 two-year-olds in the main experimental group. Twenty-one per cent, or more than one out of every five of the two-year-olds manifested active dislike for this test and only 4 per cent showed special interest in it. It is also more frequently disliked than liked by the three-year-olds, and the four-year-olds are generally indifferent toward it. The correlation with the total mental age is also lower than for test 1, especially on the first examination. There is, moreover, reason to believe that this correlation would be still lower if it were not spuriously increased through the operation of emotional factors, especially negativistic attitudes. The test is passed by 52 per cent of our two-year-olds.

Test 3 (Comprehension of directions). This test ranks high in reliability and in interest value. Its correlation with the mental-age score on the remainder of the scale is not high (.46 on the first examination) and its location in the scale appears to be too high. It was passed by 88 per cent of our two-year-olds at the time of the first test, and by 97 per cent of the same group six weeks later. It is probably worth retaining at a lower age level.

Test 4 (Drawing a circle). This test is very difficult to score consistently, a fact which probably accounts for its low reliability. There are more changes in rating, both positive and negative, from first to second test, than for any other test in the two-year series. The trouble appears to lie in part with the method of administering and scoring the test. The directions given in the manual are as follows:

(a) Place a piece of paper before the child, and make one or two rough circles on it as the child watches. Then give the child a pencil and make some more circles, as you say to the child, "You make some." Urge and repeat a number of times, if necessary.

(b) Take the child's hand with the pencil in it, and make a few rough circles for him. Release his hand and say, "Now you make some," imitating the motion above the paper at the same time.

Scoring. Passed if the child makes some effort, with sufficient success to show that he is trying to make a circle in either *a* or *b*.

It is seen that in the directions for administering, the amount of urging, the number of trials, and the amount of manual guidance are left largely to the discretion of the examiner. The scoring is also decidedly subjective, since it is frequently very hard to determine just what level of performance is to be considered as "some effort" or "sufficient success." We have scored a vertical scribble as failure, but there are many cases in which the strokes are widely separated, so that a circular scribble is approximated, and the two performances are very hard to distinguish.

In spite of its low reliability, the test correlates well with mental age. The biserial coefficient of correlation for two-year-old children was .736 on the first test and .576 on the second, and its interest value is very high. It is too difficult for our two-year-olds, of whom only 43 per cent succeed with it, but in its present form, it is too easy for age three. If manual guidance were not permitted, and the scoring were made more objective and somewhat more stringent, it would probably become an extremely useful test for three-year-olds.

Test 5 (Removal of wrapping from food before eating). The change in method of administering this test was described in Chapter II. As we have given it, the test is far too easy for our two-year-olds, of whom 96 per cent succeed with it. This is in accordance with Gesell's findings, whose procedure corresponds fairly closely to ours. Sixty per cent of his cases passed the test at 12 months, nearly all did so at 18 months. Apart from its incorrect placement, the test appears to be a good one. It is reliable and its interest value is also high. Because of the small percentage of failures, the correlation with mental age was not computed.

Three-year series.—Test 1 (Enumeration of objects in pictures). This test, which has formed a part of practically every revision of the Binet which has appeared, seems to be rather less reliable than has generally been supposed. There is a suggestion that this unreliability is, in part, a function of very slight changes in manner of administering the test, since 5 of the 6 cases of negative changes occurred when the tests were given by different examiners. It is the writer's opinion that the difficulty is in part due to the requirement that three or more objects must be named *spontaneously*, that is, without further questions or urging after the first direction has been given. The extremely docile or phlegmatic child is likely to be somewhat handicapped by this procedure, and temporary fluctuations of mood or of interest may also affect the result. Variations in the length of time allowed for response, or in the amount of urging given on the first pictures shown, are also factors in the situation, since if the child is urged to go on until he has named a large number of objects on the first picture, he is more likely to name several objects on subsequent pictures than if he is permitted to stop after naming one or two on the first, and success in a single picture is all that is required for credit. Neither the length of time permitted for response nor the amount of urging to be given is specified in the manual.

The test ranks very high in interest value and shows a rapid increase in percentage of success with increasing chronological age, a fact which is suggestive of high validity. On the two examinations, its correlation with mental age averages .61 for two- and three-year-old children taken separately. It is passed by 78 per cent of our three-year-olds.

Test 2 (Pointing out parts of the body). The change in method of giving this test was described in Chapter II. As we have given it, the test shows higher reliability than any other in the three-year series, there being only 2 cases of negative change and 17 of positive change. These all occur at the two-year level. Its interest value is also high, and its correlation with the total mental age in the case of two-year-old children was .68 on the first test and .79 on the second test. It is too easy for age three but is a very valuable test for two-year-olds. Sixty-eight per cent of our two-year-olds succeed with it. The rapid increase with age, from 68 per cent at age two to 98 per cent at age three suggests a high validity as well.

Test 3 (Giving the family name). The reliability of this test is distinctly lower than that of the two foregoing tests in the series. In our main experimental group, there were 11 instances of negative change and 24 of positive change recorded for this test. Recency of training appears to be an important factor. We have questioned the parents of a number of the children who made unexpected failures on this test and have frequently received such answers as "Why, I don't believe we've asked him to tell his name very lately. He *used* to know it," or "I had him trained so that if he got lost or anything, he could tell his name and telephone number. He could do that when he was only two, but I've been busy lately and haven't drilled him on it."

Considering its low reliability, the correlation of this test with mental age is surprisingly high, averaging .79 for the three-year-olds and .54 for the four-year-olds on the two examinations. Its interest value is low. Dislike was manifested on 4 per cent of the 774 occasions that the test was given, and positive interest on only 1 per cent. The increase with chronological age is rapid, ranging from 9 per cent of success at age two, to 62 per cent at age three, and 92 per cent at age four.

Test 4 (Repetition of a sentence of six syllables). Our main experimental group shows 13 instances of negative change and 33 of positive change in success on this test. This is the highest proportion of variability in performance recorded for any of the three-year tests. The test ranks very low in interest value, positive interest being recorded for only 2 per cent of the cases, while active dislike was manifested by 9 per cent. Emotional factors are presumably in part responsible for its unreliability. Imperfect enunciation, which often makes it difficult to determine whether or not errors in repetition have been made, renders the scoring difficult in many instances and is likely to be an additional source of unreliability. The test shows an unusually rapid increase with chronological age, from 9 per cent succeeding at age two to 61 per cent at age three, and 96 per cent at age four. The average correlation with total mental age is .69 for the three-year-old group on the two examinations.

Test 5 (Naming familiar objects). The test shows fair reliability, there being but 4 instances of negative change and 23 of positive change recorded for our group. It ranks high in interest value, especially for the two-year-olds, and in the case of the two-year-olds the correlation with mental age averages .78 for the two examinations. In difficulty, it grades about half way between the two- and three-year age levels. It is passed by 45 per cent of the two-year-olds and 90 per cent of the three-year-olds. Our data suggest that in a year scale it is worth a double credit. If two-year credit were given for three correct responses, and three-year credit for five correct responses, it would appear to be correctly placed.

Test 6 (Repeating two numerals). Apart from its low interest value (10 per cent "disliking" with only 2 per cent "liking"), the test compares well with most of the others in the series. It is more reliable than test 4, which also involves verbal repetition, and has an average correlation with mental age of .79 for two- and three-year-old children. The increase with chronological age is very rapid; 25 per cent of the two-year-olds, 85 per cent of the three-year-olds, and 100 per cent of the four-year-olds succeed with it.

Test 7 (Naming pictures from memory). This test is very reliable, there being but two instances of negative change recorded. Its interest value is also high, and its correlation with mental age is .85 for the three-year-olds and .52 for the four-year-olds. The increase with chronological age is very rapid. None of the two-year-olds and only 27 per cent of the three-year-olds succeed with it, but 83 per cent of the four-year-olds do so. The test belongs at age four rather than at age three. Apart from the error in placement it is one of the best in the series.

Test 8 (Tracing a square). This test is similar to the Porteus maze tests. Its reliability is somewhat uncertain. Only a single instance of negative change is recorded, but the number of positive changes is greater than for any other test in the three-year series. Its interest value is exceptionally high, fewer than 1 per cent of the cases showing dislike for the task as compared to 11 per cent who show positive liking for it. Its correlation with mental age averages .85 for three-year-olds but only .43 for four-year-olds. Since only 17 per cent of the three-year-olds pass the test, while 82 per cent of the four-year-olds do so, the difference in the magnitude of the correlation coefficients at the two ages may be interpreted as meaning that acceleration in a performance of this kind is a more significant indication of mental development than is retardation. The test belongs at the four-year level.

Four-year series.—Test 1 (Giving sex). Terman places this test at age three, and as 54 per cent of our three-year-olds and 89 per cent of the four-year-olds succeed with it, the three-year series would seem to be the preferable location. Its reliability is not high; there are 10 instances of negative change and 26 of positive change recorded for our main group. Neither interest nor dislike is displayed toward the test as a rule. This is probably due largely to the fact that it requires but a single word response and holds the child's attention for only an instant. Its correlation with mental age averages .73 at age three but only .43 at age four. We have sometimes suspected our four-year-olds of an attempt to play a joke upon the examiner by purposely giving a wrong answer to this test. It is difficult to check up such a suspicion without suggesting the answer, or at least implying that the first answer was incorrect, which, in this case, amounts to the same thing.

Test 2 (Repeating three numerals). This test is passed by 59 per cent of our three-year-old children and by 94 per cent of the four-year-olds. Terman places it as an alternative test at the three-year level. It is decidedly unreliable, there being 16 cases of negative and 34 of positive changes recorded for our main group. Its average correlation with mental age was .67 for three-year-old children. Its interest value is low, the ratio of "liking" to "disliking" being as 1 to 7.

Test 3 (Comparison of lines). This test, which both Terman and Kuhlman have placed at the four-year level, was passed by 14 per cent of our two-year olds, 60 per cent of the three-year-olds and 92 per cent of the four-year-olds. It appears, therefore, to belong at age three rather than at age four. In reliability it ranks decidedly low, there being 25 instances of negative and 32 of positive change recorded for our main group. It stands fairly high in interest value, less than one-half of one per cent of the cases showing active dislike for it, while positive liking was manifested by 5 per cent. At age two, it correlates with total mental age to the extent of .55; at age three the correlation is .67. Perhaps more rigid scoring would decrease the chance error; apart from its low reliability, it appears to be a valuable test.

Test 4 (Discrimination of forms). This test is one of the most reliable in the four-year series, there being but 5 instances of negative and 25 of positive change recorded for our group. It is correctly placed at age four and shows a very rapid increase with chronological age. None of the two-year-olds, 16 per cent of the three-year-olds and 73 per cent of the four-year-olds succeed with it. The correlation with mental age averages .94 on the two examinations for the three-year-olds, and .65 for four-year-olds, and it ranks higher in interest value than any of the other tests in the four-year series.

Test 5 (Tracing irregular form). This test is correctly placed at age four. It appears to be only slightly more difficult than test 8 of the three-year series, to which it closely corresponds in type. It is passed by 66 per cent of the four-year-olds, while test III 8 was passed by 82 per cent. It ranks well in interest value, with 7 per cent positive reactions and less than one-half of one per cent negative. It resembles III 8 in that the number of negative changes in success from test to test is low, and the number of positive changes high. The average correlation with mental age on the two examinations is .58 for the four-year-old group.

Test 6 (Recognition of forms). Like the foregoing, this test shows a high proportion of positive changes in success, but few negative changes. It is rather difficult for our four-year-olds, of whom only 46 per cent succeed with it. With slightly more rigid requirements, perhaps three successes out of five instead of two, it would undoubtedly scale at the five-year level. The average correlation with mental age is .66 for four-year-old children, and the interest value is high.

The required time for exposure of the small forms in this test seems to us to be too long. Even with continual urging, few of our subjects could be induced to fixate the card during the full 10 seconds. It would be well worth while to try out the results of a five-second exposure.

Test 7 (Comprehension). This test also appears to be less reliable than others in the scale. There were 12 instances of negative and 26 of positive change in our main experimental group. Its correlation with total mental age averages .55 for the four-year-olds, but its interest value is low, with 3 per cent of the cases showing dislike for it, as compared to only 1 per cent who seemed to enjoy it. It is rather easy for age four, but is better placed there than at age three, since only 38 per cent of the three-year-olds succeed with it, while 85 per cent of the four-year-olds do so.

Test 8 (Naming pictures from memory). This test is similar to test 7 in the three-year series, but is more difficult, since four pictures are used. It is rather difficult for our four-year-olds, of whom only 48 per cent succeed with it. If an additional set of pictures were used and three out of four successes required, it would perhaps scale at the five-year level. Our results show 34 instances of positive and 7 of negative changes in success in this test. Its correlation with mental age averages .60 for four-year-old children. Its interest value is very high, with 13 per cent showing positive reactions as compared to only 1 per cent of negative reactions.

Since our group included no children who were more than four-and-a-half years old, the results for the tests in the age groups above four have reference only to their value for younger children. Nevertheless, since the ratings of the three- and four-year-old children are in part determined by these tests as well as by those standardized at the earlier ages, the findings will be discussed here.

Five-year series.—Test 1 (Counting four pennies). This test, except for the final question, "How many are there?" is also used in the Stanford Revision, where it is placed at the four-year level. The addition of the final check question greatly increases the difficulty of the test, and in many cases appears to be a source of confusion to shy or timid children, who seem inclined to interpret it as an indication that their original counting was incorrect. Only 26 per cent of our four-year-olds pass the test when it is given in this form, which is a considerably lower percentage than is reported by other workers when the check question was not used. This is one of the few tests in the scale for which a greater number of negative than of positive changes in success are recorded, and these negative changes are, as a rule, traceable to failure on the check question. However, the correlation with mental age is .67 for the four-year-old children, and this compares favorably with the other tests in the year group. It has little

positive interest value, but does not arouse negativism or
other indications of active dislike.

Test 2 (Copying a square). In the Stanford Revision
this test is located at four years, but only 1 success out of 3
trials is required and the scoring is much more liberal. By
Kuhlman's requirements, only 8 per cent of our four-year-
olds succeed with it. Because of the few successes, correlation with mental age was not computed. Its reliability for
four-year-old children is not high. Of the eight cases who succeeded with it on the first test, two, or 25 per cent, failed to
score on the second test given six weeks later. The one three-
year-old child who succeeded on the first test failed six weeks
later. Its interest value is rather low, but this is probably in
part due to its difficulty for children at these early ages. Positive
enjoyment was manifested in only 2 per cent of the 664 times
that the test was given, but instances of active dislike were
also very infrequent.

Test 3 (Comparison of weights). Kuhlman's requirement
of only 4 successes out of 6 trials introduces the possibility
of chance success. In the Stanford Revision, the requirement
is two successes out of three trials, with the proviso that, in
cases where the examiner suspects chance to have played a
part, the test is to be repeated. It is our belief that the test
would be materially improved if the requirement were three
successes out of three trials or five successes out of six trials.
Our data show 36 instances of positive change and 8 of negative change among the 200 children in the three- and four-
year-old groups. The number of positive changes is higher
than for any other test in the year group. Its high correlation with mental age (.79 for three-year-old children and .58
for four-year-old children) suggests that if its reliability were
improved, it would be an unusually valuable test. It is passed
by 50 per cent of our four-year-old children and would be better placed at age four than at age five. Its interest value is

fair, with 3 per cent "liking" as compared to less than half of one per cent "disliking" it.

Test 4 (Making rectangle with two triangles). This test has been included in nearly all revisions of the Binet and has been generally placed at the five-year level. This placement is probably correct, as 30 per cent of our four-year-olds succeed with it. It ranks rather low in reliability, with 11 instances of negative and 23 of positive changes among the 200 three- and four-year-old children in the main experimental group. There is a possibility that this unreliability is in part associated with change of examiners, since 8 of the 11 instances of negative change but only 6 of the 23 instances of positive change occurred when the tests were given by different examiners. This suggests the possibility of slight differences in administrative procedure, which interfered with normal practice effect when the test was repeated.[1]

The correlation with total mental age averages .57 for four-year-old children. At this age its interest value is not high; it would probably be greater for older children. However, negativistic reactions are rare.

Test 5 (Repetition of a sentence of ten words). This test is probably more reliable than the foregoing. There were only 6 cases of negative change and 25 of positive change recorded for our three- and four-year-old children. The average correlation with mental age was .73 for three-year-olds and .59 for four-year-olds. It is disliked by 5 per cent of the cases

---

[1] At the beginning of the experiment, the examining procedure was thoroughly gone over by the two workers and methods of giving and scoring the tests were compared. Each examiner then observed about 20 complete examinations as given by the other. Doubtful points were discussed freely throughout the experiment. Subsequent checking up of the methods on this and other tests showing somewhat dissimilar results failed to reveal any differences which could be defined, but minor differences may, nevertheless, have existed.

and liked by only 2 per cent. It is passed by 50 per cent of our four-year-olds and probably belongs at this age-level rather than at age five.

Test 6 (Definition according to use of object). Our records show 9 cases of negative and 30 of positive changes in success on this test. Its correlation with mental age averages .87 for the three-year-olds and .56 for four-year-olds. Two per cent of the cases are recorded as "liking" and 1 per cent as "disliking" this test. The test has been included in practically all revisions of the Binet and has usually been located at age five. This is probably a correct placement, though 45 per cent of our four-year-olds pass it.

Test 7 (Tapping blocks in irregular order). This is a modification of the well-known Knox cube test. Kuhlman's instructions provide that the blocks are to be tapped with the forefinger rather than with a fifth cube as in the original test. Our experience indicates that the original procedure is preferable. The sharp click made by the contact of the two cubes is arresting to the child's attention and adds an element of interest which is absent when the forefinger is used.

The cubes are frequently misplaced in tapping. Punctilious children are sometimes inclined to stop and replace them before completing a series of taps. This constitutes an unfortunate interruption which may affect results. If a separate set of cubes, glued to a wooden base as in the original Knox test were substituted, this source of distraction would be removed and a more nearly uniform situation would be provided.

As given, the test shows fair reliability, there being 7 instances of negative and 32 of positive change recorded. The average correlation with mental age is .57 for four-year-old children. Positive liking is recorded for 3 per cent and active dislike by 5 per cent of the cases to whom it was given. It is passed by 41 per cent of our four-year-old children.

Test 8 (Naming the primary colors). This test, which has been quite generally located at age five is passed by 19 per cent of our four-year-olds. Its interest value for our children is higher than any other of the five-year tests. It is "liked" by 8 per cent of the cases and "disliked" by only 1 per cent. The correlation with mental age is only .39 for four-year-old children. It is comparatively reliable, there being only 4 instances of negative and 15 of positive changes recorded.

Six-year series.—Test 1 (Distinction between right and left). On the first test, 6 three-year-old children and 23 four-year-olds passed this test. On the second test, 4 of the 6 three-year-olds and 11 of the 23 four-year-olds failed with it, while 21 cases who had failed on the first occasion passed it. Chance appears to be a predominant factor in determining the result. With so low reliability the correlation with the remainder of the scale could hardly be expected to be high. It averages .31 for four-year-olds, and this is perhaps in part spurious for the reason mentioned in an earlier paragraph. The test does not seem to be worth retaining in the scale.

Test 2 (Aesthetic comparison). This test has a greater number of positive changes but fewer negative changes than the foregoing. Its correlation with mental age averages .91 for three-year-olds and .55 for four-year-olds. The high correlation at age three is in part spurious—a result of its incorrect placement at age six, so that only the brightest of the three-year-olds had a chance to try it. Terman places it at age five and requires 3 successes out of 3 trials. Kuhlman places it at age six and credits either 3 of 3 or 5 of 6 successes. It is passed by 48 per cent of our four-year-olds, and the number would probably have been greater if all had had an opportunity to try it. With the more lenient scoring method used here, it should probably be located at age four. It ranks high in interest value; with 7 per cent "liking" and none "disliking" it.

Test 3 (Distinction between morning and afternoon). On the first occasion 10 three-year-olds and 39 four-year-olds passed this test. On the second test 4 of the 10 three-year-olds and 16 of the 39 four-year-olds who had passed the test six weeks previously, failed with it; but 12 three-year-olds and 19 four-year-olds who had formerly failed, now passed it. It has been stated that children who have not actually grasped the time distinction usually repeat the last word, hence, in formulating the question the incorrect answer is always placed last. While there is undoubtedly a tendency toward this form of response in young children, our results make it appear very doubtful whether the tendency is sufficiently strong to justify the inclusion of a test of the alternative response type in a scale where high reliability is needed. The low correlation with the remainder of the scale (.36 for four-year-old children—the comparatively high figure of .83 for three-year-olds is spurious for reasons previously stated) is additional evidence of its doubtful value.

Test 4 (Recognition of mutilation in pictures). There are only 4 instances of negative change and 23 of positive change in success on this test. The average correlation with mental age is .56 for four-year-old children and its interest value is high, with 7 per cent "liking" and none "disliking" it.

Test 5 (Execution of three simultaneous commands). This test, which is placed at age six by Kuhlman, was passed by 51 per cent of our four-year-olds, and would seem, therefore, to belong at age four. It shows only fair reliability, with 8 instances of negative and 34 of positive changes. It should be noted in this connection that the commands used by Kuhlman differ from those in the Stanford Revision. The Kuhlman form of the test is "Go put that chair over there against the wall, then put this key on the chair, then close (or open) the door." The directions are repeated once. We have felt that the first command introduces an element of inconstancy into the situation, since it is not always possible to provide a chair of such size and weight that a small child can move it without effort when testing is done outside the regular laboratory. It is, of course, true that no great effort is required from the child even if an ordinary adult-size chair is used; nevertheless, the comparative inconvenience of the task may, by serving as a distraction, affect his performance on the two remaining commands.

The test ranks exceptionally high in interest value, with 14 per cent of the cases "liking" it, as opposed to only 1 per cent who "dislike" it. The correlation with mental age averages .61 for the four-year-old children on the two examinations.

Test 6 (Counting irregular series of four to six taps). For our children, this test is the most difficult one in the six-year series. None of the three-year-olds and only 4 of the four-year-old children passed it on the first examination, and 3 of these failed to pass it on the second examination, while 7 additional cases who failed to pass it on the first occasion did so on the second.

Test 7 (Folding a square of paper three times). This test was passed by 14 of our four-year-olds on the first occasion but 6 of these failed to pass it six weeks later. It correlates with mental age to the extent of .62 in the case of four-year-old children and ranks fairly high in interest value, with 4 per cent "liking" it and 1 per cent "disliking."

Test 8 (Tapping blocks in irregular order). This test is similar to test V 7, except for the increase in difficulty. It is passed by 15 per cent of our four-year-olds. There are 4 instances of negative and 13 of positive changes recorded. It correlates with mental age to the extent of .65 with four-year-old children, but ranks rather low in interest value with 4 per cent "disliking" and only 3 per cent "liking" it.

Seven-year series.—Test 1 (Picture description). This test is passed by 23 per cent of our four-year-old children. It is very probable that the change in manner of adminstering the test is in part responsible for this high percentage. Unless the rate of increase with age is much less rapid than for most tests in the scale, it seems highly probable that the test really belongs in the five-year, or at most, in the six-year series. Its reliability is only fair; there are 9 instances of negative and 23 of positive changes recorded for it. Its interest value is high, with 8 per cent "liking" it and none "disliking," but the correlation with mental age on the remainder of the scale is comparatively low—only .38 for four-year-old children.

Test 2 (Naming the first four coins). This test was passed by 1 three-year-old child and by 8 four-year-olds on the first examination, but 5 of these 9 children failed to pass it on the second examination. It was "liked" by 3 per cent of the cases and "disliked" by less than half of 1 per cent.

Test 3 (Telling the number of fingers). None of our cases passed this test on either examination.

Test 4 (Repetition of five numerals). This test was passed by 20 per cent of our four-year-olds and by 2 of the three-year-olds on the first examination, which suggests that it may be standardized at too high a level. There were only 4 instances of negative change, but 28 of positive change recorded for our group. Its interest value is low, with 4 per cent of the cases "disliking" it and only 2 per cent "liking" it. Its correlation with mental age is rather high, averaging .60 for the four-year-olds on the two examinations.

Test 5 (Comparing two objects from memory). Only 3 of our four-year-olds passed this test on the first examination, and 2 of these failed to pass it six weeks later, at which time it was passed by 3 additional cases.

Test 6 (Giving word opposites). This test was passed by one four-year-old child on the first examination, who failed, however, to pass it on the second occasion. Four other children passed it at this time.

Tests 7-8 (Repeating three numerals backward and drawing a diamond from copy). None of our cases passed these tests on either of the two occasions.

Eight-year series.—None of the tests in this series were passed by any of the children in our groups on the first examination. On the second examination, tests V and VI (word opposites and giving similarities) were each passed by one child in the four-year group.

CHAPTER V

ADDITIONAL FACTORS AFFECTING THE RELIABILITY OF THE SCALE

The data presented in the foregoing chapters have to do with the general reliability of the scale as an instrument for the measurement of mental development in children of pre-school age. The question of possible fluctuations in mental growth-rate, and the effect of varying emotional attitudes upon test performance will be discussed briefly in the sections which follow.

FLUCTUATIONS IN MENTAL GROWTH-RATE

Changes in the growth-rate of individuals.—Our data are in-adequate to determine the extent to which variations in indi-vidual mental growth-rate are likely to occur, owing to the comparatively brief interval between the two tests and the ir-regularities in the standardization of the scale, which were pointed out in Chapters III and IV. Even were these diffi-culties not present it is doubtful whether or not fluctua-tions other than those of a very gross nature extending over a considerable period of time or involving actual mental de-terioration can be detected by the instruments now available. It must be remembered that our units of mental measurements are not absolute terms such as feet or inches, but relative; that they have no meaning in and of themselves, but merely serve to relate the performance of an individual to that of a supposedly typical group of the same age.

Apart from all questions of instrumental error, changes in mental growth-rate cannot be determined by our present methods unless these changes take the form of personal idiosyncrasies or are related to some constant factor or factors, the presence or absence of which is known. We do not know, for example, how the absolute amount of growth from age two to age three compares with that from age three to age four. We can only say that certain intellectual tasks can be performed by the average child at the age of two while certain others cannot, as a rule, be accomplished until three or four; and on the basis of these observed facts, it is possible to determine the general level of performance most typical of any given age, i.e., to establish a series of mental-age norms. These norms, however, cannot be directly compared with each other, since there is no reason for believing that the quantitative differences between the successive developmental steps are equal. Moreover, since the scales are made up of a large number of different elements in which the time normally required to accomplish the gain from step to step varies greatly according to the type of material used[1] (compare Table 20), unusual proficiency or deficiency in one or another of these special types of performance affects the total rating to an unequal extent at different periods of development. It appears obvious, therefore, that individual changes in rating may be due to any of a rather large number of different causes which are inherent in the method employed for measurement rather than in the individual measured.

Even though all of the separate items in a test were perfectly reliable in a statistical sense and though a maximum degree of cooperation were invariably obtained from all subjects, it would still be unsafe to assume that temporary fluctuations in obtained ratings represent actual changes in the rate

[1] In the absence of absolute scales of measurement, it is, of course, impossible to determine whether these differences are due to actual differences in the rate of development of different mental functions or to unequal spacing of the measured steps. The effect upon the mental rating is the same in either case.

of development of the individual rather than inequalities in the distribution throughout the scale of tasks of different types, or of those in which the stages measured are unequally spaced for difficulty. It would appear, therefore, that a reliable determination of the presence or absence of individual changes in mental growth-rate must wait upon the development of more precise instruments than any which are now available.[2]

Changes in the mental growth-rate of selected groups.—In spite of these difficulties and others of a similar nature, it is nevertheless at least theoretically possible, provided certain specific requirements can be met, to determine the effect of artificially imposed conditions upon the rate of mental growth, as this is measured by intelligence tests. These requirements may be enumerated briefly as follows: (1) the factor to be considered must be subject to objective measurement and experimental control, (2) all individuals should be measured both before and after the experimental period, (3) a sufficient number of cases must be included in the experiment to give statistical reliability to the results, and (4) the findings should be further verified by comparison with a control group known to be similar to the group under consideration in all essential respects except the trait to be studied.

If the first condition is unsatisfactorily met, relationships actually existing may become obscured as a result of imperfect segregation of groups varying in regard to the characteristic studied, while the personal prejudices or emotional bias of the investigator may lead to such a classification of the data as to give apparent support to erroneous conclusions. Unless measurement of the same individuals both before and after the experimental period is possible, it is necessary to exercise extreme caution in the interpretation of data based upon comparisons between groups whose original standing is unknown.

[2] Except, of course, in certain types of distinctly pathological cases.

Equal conservatism becomes necessary when some cases drop out in the course of the experiment so that not all are included in the final measurement. Unless it can be shown that the eliminative factors are unrelated to the field of measurement, it is unsafe to assume that changes in the group ratings are due to factors experimentally introduced rather than to selective elimination.

At first thought, it may seem that if selective elimination could be avoided, and if the subjects were measured both before and after the experimental period, that a special control group would become unnecessary. This would be true only if the experimental group were known to constitute a strictly representative sampling of the general population, and adequate growth norms for such a group were available. Under those circumstances, the required control factor is effectively provided by the norms themselves, unless the factor under consideration or some correlated factor has been operative in the establishment of those norms. For example, it is obviously impossible to determine whether school training affects the results of an intelligence test by comparing the intelligence quotients of unselected individuals at the time of school entrance with those earned after a period of school attendance, since any effect which the training may have had would presumably have entered into the performance of the individuals used in the original standardization to an equally marked degree.

Variations in normative standards may come about in many ways, and quite unexpected results are not infrequently obtained through their uncritical acceptance as a final basis for comparison. As an illustration, we may take the case of an intelligence test standardized upon school children just before the age limit of compulsory attendance was increased from fourteen to sixteen years. Since, on the average, the children who remain in school beyond the compulsory attendance limit represent a distinctly higher intellectual class than those who leave, it is almost certain that the norms for the ages above fourteen would be much too high, and that as a result the change in the attendance law would bring into school a large number of children spuriously rated as very backward. Moreover, the intelligence quotients of younger bright children would be expected to undergo a sudden drop at the point where the mental ages coincide with the change in the composition of the original age groups. Since in actual practice, it is rarely possible to ascertain how closely a given experimental group corresponds to that used in the derivation of norms, the use of a special control group upon which comparisons may be based is obviously desirable. The validity of the conclusions drawn from such a comparison will then rest upon the degree of fundamental similarity of the two groups in the outset, and the extent to which experimental conditions have been controlled.

Effect of nursery-school training upon intelligence-test performance.[3]—The method just described has been used in an attempt to determine whether environmental stimulation of the kind provided by the nursery school has any appreciable effect upon intelligence-test scores. The data are based upon a comparison of changes in IQ of a group of 28 children after a year's attendance at the nursery school conducted by the Institute of Child Welfare, University of Minnesota, with the corresponding changes in an equal number of paired controls. As regards age, the nursery-school children are divided into two distinct groups: a younger group, whose ages at the time of school entrance ranged from 2 years, 0 months, to 2 years, 6 months, and an older group, whose ages at entrance ranged

[3] See "A preliminary report on the effect of nursery-school training upon the intelligence-test ratings of young children" by Florence L. Goodenough in the *Year Book of the National Society for the Study of Education*, 1927 (Vol. 1.).

from 3 years, 3 months, to 4 years, 2 months. In home background and social status they rank somewhat above the average of our main experimental group. Fifty-four per cent of the cases are drawn from occupational groups I and II and only 7 per cent from groups V and VI. These children were tested with the Kuhlman Revision for the first time about six weeks before the opening of the nursery school, and the second test was given within a week after entrance. A third test was given near the end of the school year. Each of the nursery-school children was paired off against another child, not in the nursery school, who had been given two examinations during the fall in the course of the main study. These children were also given a third examination after an interval equal to that which had elapsed in the case of the nursery-school children. Pairing was made on the basis of the following characteristics: sex, age, IQ on each of the first two tests, interval between tests, paternal occupation, education of parents, and nativity of parents.

The results have been presented in detail in the article cited. They may be summarized briefly as follows. The mean IQ found by averaging the results of the first two tests given to the younger group of nursery-school children was 112.5 and for the control group of the same age, 112.6. On the third test, which was given approximately six months after the second test, the mean IQs were 122.4 for the nursery-school children and 120.6 for the control group. The nursery-school children made an average gain of 9.9 points of IQ; the control group 8.0 points. The older group of nursery-school children earned a mean rating of 115.6 on the first two tests, and of 128.1 on the third test; the control group means were 116.8 on the first two tests and 125.6 on the third test. The nursery-school children in this age group gained on the average 12.5 points of IQ; the control group 8.8 points. The differences are in favor of the nursery-school children in each instance, but they are so small as to be well within the limits of chance. The two greatest individual gains were made by control-group children, and the three greatest individual losses also occurred among the control group.

A second check upon the effects of the nursery-school training is afforded by the correlation between actual number of days' attendance at school and gain or loss in IQ. These correlations were calculated for the two groups of nursery-school children. The total range of attendance for the younger group was from 27 to 111 days, with the mean at 73 days and standard deviation of 25.7 days. The correlation between gain in IQ and number of days' attendance was $+.279$. The attendance of the older group of children ranged from 50 to 109 days, with the mean at 87 days and standard deviation of 14.8 days. For this group, the correlation between gain in IQ and number of days' attendance was $-.009$. Since there were only 14 cases in each group, neither of these correlations can be regarded as significant.

The question of the effect of training was also considered with reference to possible qualitative changes in order of development of specific functions, as indicated by the comparative percentages of success and failure on the individual tests made by children in the nursery school and those in the control group. The scale was also gone over with the nursery-school teachers, who rated each test according to the extent to which, in their judgment, it was likely to be affected by the special activities of the nursery-school curriculum. No differences which could be regarded as significant were found.

Because of the small number of cases and the relatively brief duration of the training period, the results which have been reported justify only the most tentative conclusions. There is, however, no valid indication that environmental stimulation of the kind afforded by this particular nursery school for the length of time considered had any appreciable effect upon intelligence-test performance. Later findings with a larger number of cases and a more protracted period of training may show changes which are not at present apparent. The data obtained in this brief study are of value chiefly as an illustration of the extent to which spurious factors may operate to give an appearance of changes in the mental-growth curve which do not exist in fact, and to point the need for rigid control of experimental conditions if valid conclusions are to be reached.

The relation of length of interval between tests to changes in IQ.—Since the interval between the first and second test was so brief, the data can be considered as significant only in regard to the question of direct memory, or practice effect in a rather limited sense. It is reasonable to suppose that the shorter the interval, the more effective would be the recall, and that accordingly a negative correlation might be found between length of interval and gain. Table 23 shows the correlation between length of interval and gain in IQ, also between length of interval and absolute change, without regard to its direction, for the 380 cases in the total retest group. The range of intervals between tests for this group is from 4 to 18 weeks.

TABLE 23

CORRELATION BETWEEN DIFFERENCES IN IQ RATINGS ON THE TWO TESTS AND
LENGTH OF INTERVAL BETWEEN TESTS
(Total Reset Group)

	Age 2	Age 3	Age 4	Total
	Cases 122	126	132	380
Algebraic difference and interval	r —.201	+.172	+.365	+.111
	P.E. ±.059	±.060	±.058	±.035
	Cases 122	126	132	380
Absolute difference (disregarding sign) and interval	r —.024	+.045	—.322	—.104
	P.E. ±.060	±.063	±.058	±.035

None of the correlations obtained at ages two and three

are large enough to be significant. At age four, the correlations are approximately six times the probable error, but the relationship is the opposite of that which was to be expected on the basis of the foregoing hypothesis. The explanation probably lies in the spurious increase in rating with age, to which attention has previously been called.

Further evidence as to the relationship between length of interval and change in IQ is afforded by a comparison of the rank-order correlations between the IQs earned on the first two examinations and those earned on the second and third for the 56 cases who were given a third test. Since no significant differences were found between the nursery-school children and the paired controls as regards tendency to gain or lose in IQ rating, the two classes have been thrown together, but the age groups have been kept separate. It is reasonable to suppose that, since the interval between the first and second tests was less than one-fourth as great as that between the second and third, changes in growth-rate would be more likely to occur during the latter interval than during the former, and that corresponding differences in the magnitude of the correlation coefficients might thereby result. Table 24 shows the correlations between the IQs earned on the three successive tests.

TABLE 24

RANK ORDER CORRELATION BETWEEN IQs EARNED ON THREE SUCCESSIVE TESTS

	Tests 1-2	Tests 1-3	Tests 2-3
Younger group (28 cases)	.693	.763	.820
Older group (28 cases)	.940	.844	.835

The results expressed in Table 24 are somewhat ambiguous, due to the small number of cases included in each group. Changes in the relative positions of the various members of the group with respect to each other are apparently more frequent among the younger group of children than among the older ones, and this is in accordance with data presented in the foregoing chapters. But the differences in the correlations obtained between successive tests for the same age-groups are well within the limits of chance; and if the mean values for the two age-groups are considered, they are practically identical. There is no evidence that fluctuations in development of such magnitude or frequency that the predictive value of the IQ would be seriously invalidated thereby have occurred in these groups within the period of time considered.

THE EFFECT OF EMOTIONAL ATTITUDES UPON INTELLIGENCE TEST PERFORMANCE

Method of Approach.—Since no objective means for the measurement of emotional attitudes which could be used during the test situation has been devised, the only practicable method appeared to be a rating scale. This method is open to many obvious criticisms, which need not be gone into here. It is, however, unquestionably superior to the "general impressions" or "personal opinion" which have formed the basis for most of the discussion of this question up to the present time, since such impressions are all too frequently based upon the recollection of one or two outstanding cases rather than upon an impartial survey of an unselected group. The exceptional is then likely to be confused with the usual, and the nature of the conclusions is determined chiefly by personal bias. While it is of course quite impossible to do away completely with the subjective element in rating, the method unquestionably has the following advantages as compared to the "general impression":

1. The ratings are made at the time of testing, thus avoiding errors due to lapses of memory.

2. They are based upon overt behavior, defined in as objective terms as possible.

3. Conclusions may be based upon an unprejudiced examination and summary of all the data for all the cases, and need not be unduly weighted by the memory of a few outstanding examples.

For the purposes of this study it was felt that no advantage would be gained by an attempt at over-fine discrimination as to modes of behavior. It was found possible, however, to distinguish at least three fairly well-defined behavior-traits which were believed to be symptomatic of emotional states or attitudes that might be expected to affect the test performance. These traits will be referred to as *shyness*, *negativism*, and *distractibility*. It is of course recognized that, particularly in the case of the first two, the underlying emotional factor may frequently be the same, but since the overt behavior-manifestations are quite different, it was felt that it would be desirable to make the distinction. Ratings on all three traits were recorded for all cases at the time of testing. A further rating on *general cooperativeness* was given, which included not only a sort of weighted estimate of the combined effect upon test performance of the traits just mentioned, but also took into consideration the apparent degree of interest and effort and any other pertinent factors.

Shyness or timidity.—Ratings on this trait were given as follows: A rating of 3 to those children who, on being first brought to the examining room, cried or clung tightly to the mother, refused to look at toys or to speak, and in whom some residual effect of the initial reaction, indicated by mydriasis of pupils, tendency to whisper responses, unwillingness to have mother leave the room, or anxiety as to her whereabouts if she did so, persisted throughout the examination. A rating of 2 was given to children who required more than the usual time to adjust to the situation in the beginning, but who showed no indications of real fear, and who, once the preliminary adjustments had been made, talked freely, did not object to having the mother leave the room, and in whom no residual effect of the initial behavior could be observed thereafter. Children who came to the examining room readily without the mother, or who were willing to have the mother leave the room within a moment or two, and who appeared entirely at ease throughout the tests were given a rating of 1.

A summary of the data on this trait for the 380 cases in the total retest group[4] reveals a number of interesting points. The correlations of the ratings given on the two examinations are surprisingly high; roughly calculated by the method of unlike-signed pairs, the coefficients appear to be above .9 for each of the three age-groups when the tests are given by the same examiner, and but slightly lower when there was a change of examiner. The ratings on the second test tend to be lower (indicating less shyness) than those on the first, which was of course to be expected. There is some improvement with age. On the first test, 65 per cent of the two-year-olds, 75 per cent of the three-year-olds, and 82 per cent of the four-year-olds were given a rating of 1. On the second test, however, the age difference practically disappears, with 86 per cent of the two-year-olds, 84 per cent of the three-year-olds, and 89 per cent of the four-year-olds rated 1. Fewer than 5 per cent of the cases at any age were rated 3 on either examination. No sex differences and no relationship between shyness and paternal occupation were found.

The correlation between change in IQ and change in rating on shyness was calculated for the three age-groups separately. At age two the correlation was found to be $+.339$; at age three, $+.125$; at age four, $+.572$. The average is $+.355$. Since the data for both variables are derived through the use of fallible measuring instruments, the true relationship is presumably

[4] This number does not include the 15 cases whose cooperation was so clearly unsatisfactory that the test results have not been included in any part of the statistical treatment. See page 13.

in excess of that indicated by the figures just given. The point of immediate practical importance, however, is this: that at least for the two examiners who took part in this study, *the accuracy of a prediction as to change in IQ, based upon observed changes in behavior as here described, would be but little better than sheer guess* (k=.874).

Negativism.—This form of behavior was frequently, though by no means invariably, an accompaniment of that which we have classified as "shyness," but it also appeared in children who showed no indications of shyness as we have defined the term. Ratings were given as follows: A rating of 3 when the child responded to more than half the tests by saying "No," or "I don't want to," or by silence, so that cooperation could be secured only by the aid of much urging, subterfuge, bribery, or similar methods. A rating of 2 was given to children who showed opposition to certain tests in the scale, but in general responded readily. Children who responded promptly throughout the examination, and were willing at least to attempt whatever they were asked to do were given a rating of 1.

As with the foregoing trait, the correlations between the ratings on the two examinations are very high (averaging above .9) and are slightly higher when both tests are given by the same examiner than when there is a change of examiners. Age differences are in the same direction and, on the first test, about equal in amount to those reported for shyness, but contrary to the findings on the former trait, these differences do not disappear when the second test is given, and there is only a small amount of improvement from test to test at any age.

There is apparently a sex difference. The mean rating for the boys is higher (indicating greater tendency to negativism) than is that for the girls at every age on the first test, and at ages three and four on the second test. When the data are subjected to further analysis, however, the gross sex difference is found to be secondary to a social difference, which operates unequally for the two sexes. Among the boys, the greatest amount of negativism is found in the upper occupational classes. This is clearly true for ages two and three on both tests; at age four the differences are less apparent because of the relatively infrequent appearance of this form of behavior at that age. Even there, however, the mean rating of Groups I, II, and III combined is higher (more negativistic) than the mean of Groups IV, V, and VI combined, on each of the two examinations. For the total group of boys, the means for the successive occupational classes are 1.56, 1.85, 1.44, 1.28, 1.08, and 1.17 on the first test and 1.47, 1.36, 1.27, 1.19, 1.08, and 1.09 on the second test. The difference between the mean rating of the first three classes and that of the last three is more than three times the standard error of the difference for both examinations. This fact, taken in conjunction with the consistency of the findings for the three age-groups on the two examinations, leaves little room for doubt that the difference is a true one.

The findings for the girls are very different. There is no very consistent difference between the social classes in respect to this trait, though there is some indication of a trend in the opposite direction to that which was found for the boys, i.e., more negativism among the children whose fathers belong to the lower occupational groups. The differences are, however, within the limits of chance. When the sexes within the same occupational groups are compared with each other, it is found that in Groups I, II, and III the boys show more negativism than the girls; no sex difference is discernible in Group IV, and in Groups V and VI the girls are more negativistic than the boys. These facts are shown graphically in Figure VII.

FIGURE VII

MEAN RATINGS ON NEGATIVISM BY SEX AND PATERNAL OCCUPATION

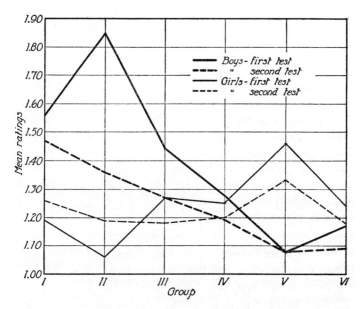

It is interesting to compare these findings with a report by
Levy and Tulchin.[5] In a group of 561 cases ranging in age
from six months to five years, they found the females to be
more resistant than the males at all ages except at thirty
months. Their cases were obtained almost entirely from the
lower occupational classes, farmers and miners predominat-
ing. Their data lead them to the conclusion that resistance
is an innate behavior reaction. Taken in a literal sense this
can hardly be doubted; nevertheless, the finding of such well-

[5] David Levy and S. Tulchin, "The Resistance of Infants and Children During Mental Tests," *Journal of Experimental Psychology*, Vol. 6
(1923), pp. 304-322 and Vol. 8 (1925), pp. 209-224.

marked differences between social classes, together with the fact that these differences are distributed in so dissimilar a fashion between the two sexes renders it very difficult to escape the conclusion that, at least in its overt manifestations, the reaction is one which is highly subject to modification by training.

Correlations between changes in the ratings on negativism and changes in IQ from first to second test were as follows: at age two, $+.417$; at age three, $+.187$; at age four, $+.465$. The average is $+.356$.

Distractibility.—A rating of 3 was given to those children whose attention could not be kept upon one thing for more than a few seconds at a time. These children, as a rule, were hyperactive, continually jumping up from the table and running to inspect something in the room, pulling out drawers of the desk, or snatching materials. A toy would be glanced at or handled for an instant, then thrown aside. Continual chattering on irrelevant subjects was a characteristic form of behavior of the older children in this group. A rating of 2 was given to children who showed greater control of physical activity than those just described; i.e., for the most part remained in their chairs or at least standing by the table, but who were unusually likely to be diverted by noises from the hall or by a chance sight of the contents of a desk drawer, and who showed only momentary persistence at any given task. Children who remained quietly seated during the examination, gave good attention to directions, and were not unduly distracted by outside stimuli were given a rating of 1.

The correlations between the ratings on the two successive examinations average .8 and are apparently not at all affected by a change of examiners. The ratings show only a slight tendency to improve from test to test, but this tendency is consistent for both sexes and at all ages. Both age and sex differences are apparent; the younger children of both sexes being rated as more distractible than the older ones and the boys more distractible than the girls. No consistent relationship between this trait and paternal occupation was established.

There is no indication that, as the test situation was handled, behavior of this sort affects the IQ adversely. The correlations between change in rating and change in IQ were −.273 at age two; −.075 at age three, and +.082 at age four. These are all within the limits of chance. The practice of both examiners was not to attempt to restrain the over-active, excitable child too rigidly, but rather to seize upon a favorable moment for presenting each test, make certain that the attention was gained and held for the time being, and to permit almost unlimited freedom of activity between the tests.

General cooperativeness.—Since these ratings were intended to represent a composite estimate of a rather large number of different factors, it was thought best not to attempt specific definition of the several steps, but to use instead a series of simple descriptive terms which would permit the examiner to base her rating upon the total behavior of the child during the test situation. Ratings were given as follows: excellent, good, fair, poor, very poor.

The self-correlations of the ratings on the two examinations are somewhat lower than was found for the more specifically defined traits. The average for the three age-groups is .600. The correlations are somewhat higher when the tests are given by the same examiner on both occasions, than when there is a change of examiners, the comparative figures being .673 and .527. Since the means and standard deviations of the ratings by the two examiners agree very closely, it would appear that the difference is to be attributed largely if not entirely to a difference in the relative importance which was ascribed to the various modes of behavior by the two examiners, i.e., to a difference in weighting.

The ratings on the second examination show an improvement in cooperativeness as compared to the first at all ages and for both sexes. At ages three and four, the girls are rated as more cooperative than the boys, but at age two the difference is in favor of the boys. This may be a true difference, since Levy found that for his cases the age of maximum resistance to the test situation was 18 months for the girls and 30 months for the boys. Some relationship between these ratings and paternal occupation is apparent. The differences are less marked than was found in the case of negativism, but they follow the same pattern and probably indicate the extent to which negativism has affected the ratings.

Correlations between change in rating on cooperativeness and change in IQ are positive but low. At age two the correlation was $+.135$; at age three, $+.100$; at age four, $+.271$. These correlations are lower than was found for either shyness or negativism considered separately. It seems probable that the lower reliability of these ratings as compared to those for the traits which were more rigidly defined in the outset may be in part responsible for these low figures. It was stated in an earlier paragraph that precise definitions were avoided in this instance because it was felt desirable to leave the examiner free to base his ratings not only upon the usual types of behavior which might be included in a definition, but also upon unusual forms not unlikely to be foreseen or defined, but which might, nevertheless, have considerable bearing upon the outcome. The results obtained suggest that objectivity of definition, even at the risk of too narrow limitation of meaning, is a desideratum of first importance in a rating system.

Diurnal variations in test efficiency.—Among the many studies dealing with the effects of fatigue upon mental work, there have been few which have considered the question of possible diurnal variation in the ability to perform tasks of the kind included in the ordinary intelligence test, and none, so far as the writer is aware, in which the subjects have been children of preschool age. Such studies are obviously needed, since at these early ages emotional control is so little developed as to render it highly unsafe to generalize upon the basis of experimental work carried out with older children or with adults.

Our study is not well adapted to determining the likelihood of the occurrence of diurnal variation in test performance for two reasons. In the first place, since it was desired to study the reliability of the tests when given under conditions as nearly optimum as could be obtained, a special effort was made to schedule all examinations at such an hour that the child's daily routine would be as little disturbed as possible. This resulted in a much greater number of tests being given at certain preferred hours, while at other hours the number of tests was so small that no conclusions would be justified. Moreover, since the factors limiting the hours at which tests could be given were not the same for all sources of supply, it became necessary in treating the data to make a further subdivision on this basis, with the result that the number of cases upon which the separate determinations are based has been still further reduced. Because of the inequalities in standardization of the scale, and the difference in normal practice effect at different ages, separate treatment of the results for the various age-groups would have been desirable, but the size of our group did not warrant this division. With the exception of the early afternoon hours, however, at which an unduly large proportion of four-year-old children whose afternoon-nap habit had been discontinued were examined, the examinations are distributed over the day without reference to age, hence it is unlikely that combining ages has had any material effect upon the results obtained.

Table 25 shows the mean IQs earned by children examined at various hours of the day. In this table, Group A includes

TABLE 25

MEANS AND STANDARD DEVIATIONS OF IQs EARNED BY CHILDREN WHO WERE EXAMINED AT DIFFERENT HOURS OF THE DAY
(Total Retest Group)

					Hour of beginning test				
	8:30-9:25	9:30-10:25	10:30-11:25	11:30-12:25	12:30-1:25	1:30-2:25	2:30-3:25	3:30-4:25	4:30-5:25
TEST 1									
Group A									
Cases	24	40	44	2	0	32	39	21	2
Mean IQ	109.9	109.8	110.2	94.5	....	112.6	109.6	111.6	114.5
S.D.	13.5	16.6	16.0	10.0	....	17.2	13.9	15.5	10.0
Group B									
Cases	6	37	34	5	0	1	4	3	0
Mean IQ	101.2	101.0	102.4	102.5	....	105.0	97.0	104.5	....
S.D.	14.9	19.5	15.9	19.4	....	....	16.4	21.6	....
Group C									
Cases	5	18	16	1	4	32	10	0	0
Mean IQ	106.5	103.9	105.1	105.0	112.0	105.1	112.5	....	....
S.D.	9.8	8.5	16.4	....	10.9	10.6	16.8	....	....
TEST 2									
Group A									
Cases	32	38	51	5	1	25	21	28	3
Mean IQ	118.9	113.2	113.5	100.5	115.0	120.1	112.6	126.3	124.5
S.D.	21.2	20.3	16.6	10.2	....	19.6	15.0	14.1	24.5
Group B									
Cases	10	54	16	1	0	0	5	4	0
Mean IQ	108.5	107.3	100.8	85.0	....	....	92.5	82.0	....
S.D.	22.2	17.3	19.8	....	....	....	7.5	6.1	....
Group C									
Cases	3	20	11	3	10	30	6	3	0
Mean IQ	111.2	102.5	105.4	124.5	105.5	114.8	106.2	101.2	....
S.D.	17.0	12.5	13.8	28.2	13.0	15.6	12.2	5.7	....

114

all cases examined at the Institute laboratory; Group B includes cases examined at day nurseries and the orphanage
group; Group C, cases examined at the Infant Welfare Clinics. Each of these groups is homogeneous so far as factors
limiting the hours at which examinations could be made are
concerned.

Examination of Table 25 shows no reliable differences
between the IQs earned by children of similar supply groups
who were examined at different hours. The afternoon ratings
tend to be slightly higher than those made during the morning, but this difference is almost certainly spurious, a result
of the excess of four-year-old children tested at that time, for
whom the established norms are especially lenient. While
it would not be safe to assume, on the basis of these findings,
that the hour of the day at which a preschool-age child is
examined has no bearing whatever upon the quality of his
performance, it appears that, granted such precautions as were
observed in this study, the hour of the examination is at most
a factor of very minor importance. This conclusion is further borne out by a study of the changes in IQ earned by the
same children when the two examinations were given at different hours. There is no one hour which appears to be consistently superior to any other hour. Nevertheless, the possibility that a greater number of cases or a more adequate
measuring instrument might have revealed differences which
are not at present apparent is suggested by the fact that when
the arithmetic mean of the changes in IQ earned by the 109
cases in the total retest group who were given both examinations at the same hour is compared with the corresponding
figure for the 271 cases whose second examination was given
at a different hour from the first, it is found that the latter
group shows a mean variation of 10.4 points of IQ as compared to 8.5 points for the group who were given both tests
at the same hour. The difference is 2.29 times its standard

error and would occur by chance only about once in one hundred times.

SUMMARY

1. The possibilities and limitations of intelligence tests as instruments for detecting the presence of fluctuations in the mental growth-rate of individuals and of selected groups are discussed.

2. Changes in the IQs of a group of 28 children after a year's attendance at a nursery school are compared with the corresponding changes in an equal number of children selected to resemble the nursery-school children in respect to age, sex, IQ at the beginning of the study, paternal occupation, education of parents, and nativity of parents. Intervals between tests were the same for both groups. The results do not warrant the assumption that environmental stimulation of the kind considered in this study has any appreciable effect upon the rate of mental growth.

3. The relationship of length of interval between tests to change in IQ is considered. No significant relationship was found within the limits of interval employed in this study (4 to 32 weeks).

4. Ratings on certain forms of emotional behavior as displayed during the test situation were given to all children at the time of testing. Separate ratings were given on each of the following traits: shyness, negativism, distractibility, and general cooperativeness. A summary of the results shows that the ratings on the first three traits were highly reliable, in the sense that there was little change in the ratings for the same individual on the two examinations, while those on the fourth trait were somewhat less reliable; that there is some improvement with age on all four traits as well as a general tendency to improvement from first to second examination. Correlations between change in rating and change in IQ average $+.355$ for

shyness, $+.356$ for negativism, $-.089$ for distractibility, and $+.169$ for general cooperativeness. No sex difference could be detected with regard to shyness. Apparent sex differences in negativism were shown to be secondary to social differences in the behavior of the sexes. In occupational groups I, II, and III the boys were more negativistic than the girls, in group IV, no sex difference could be detected, and in groups V and VI the girls were more negativistic than the boys, though the latter difference was not statistically reliable. The boys were somewhat more distractible than the girls. In general cooperativeness the girls were superior to the boys at ages three and four, while at age two the boys were superior to the girls.

5. Diurnal variation in mental efficiency as a possible factor influencing the test results was considered both with regard to the mean IQs earned by children who were examined at different hours of the day, and with regard to changes in IQ from first to second test when these tests were given at different hours. The results do not indicate that diurnal variation of such magnitude as to affect the results of the test in any practically significant degree is likely to occur, provided that the child's habitual routine of meals and sleep is not interfered with, though there is a suggestion that minor variations may be present. Further investigation of the question is needed.

CHAPTER VI

EXTREME CHANGES IN IQ

Examination of the records for the 380 cases in the total retest group reveals a total of 14 instances in which the gain in rating from first to second test amounted to 25 or more points of IQ, while at the other extreme there are 15 cases which showed a loss of 12 points or more. It was thought that a comparison of the data for these two groups of cases might serve to throw additional light upon the causes of variability in rating. For convenience in presenting the data, the first group will be referred to as Group A; the second as Group B.

Age.—Group A includes 1 two-year-old, 7 three-year-olds, and 6 four-year-olds; Group B includes 7 two-year-olds, 6 three-year-olds, and 2 four-year-olds. It is evident that marked loss in rating occurs most frequently among the younger children, while extreme gains are found more often among the older ones.

Sex.—Group A includes 6 boys and 8 girls; Group B, 11 boys and 4 girls. Large gains are slightly more frequent among the girls, marked losses among the boys. This is quite possibly a function of the age factor rather than a true sex difference, since it might readily result from an unequal distribution throughout the scale of tests which favor one or the other sex.

Paternal occupation.—The distribution for the two groups is shown below:

	I	II	III	IV	V	VI
Group A	6	2	4	0	1	1
Group B	1	0	3	5	2	4

The tendency for children coming from the higher occupational classes to gain while those from the lower classes are more likely to lose is clearly seen in this group of extreme cases.

IQ earned on first test.—The distributions for the two groups follow:

	60–69	70–79	80–89	90–99	100–109	110–119	120–129	130–139	Mean
Group A	1	1	0	4	1	4	2	1	104.5
Group B	1	0	2	2	4	4	2	0	103.2

Without correction for regression, no relationship between original IQ and gain or loss in rating is indicated. It is obvious that a prediction as to probable increase or decrease in rating on subsequent tests is much more reliable if based upon paternal occupation than upon the original IQ.

Examiners.—The distribution of examiners for the two groups is shown below:

	A–A	B–B	A–B	B–A
Group A	1	5	5	3
Group B	2	4	3	6
Total	3	9	8	9

There is a suggestion that marked variations are more likely to occur in the tests made by Examiner B, who was the less experienced of the two, than in those made by Examiner A. It should be noted, however, that extreme variations in both directions occur under each of the four circumstances.

Changes in behavior during tests.—These changes have been summarized below. A higher rating, as the term is used here, indicates an improvement in the behavior as rated; a lower rating indicates a change for the worse.

	Higher	No change	Lower
Cooperativeness			
Group A	3	11	0
Group B	4	6	5
Shyness			
Group A	1	12	1
Group B	3	8	4
Negativism			
Group A	2	12	0
Group B	2	10	3
Distractibility			
Group A	1	12	1
Group B	2	9	4
Total for four ratings			
Group A	7	47	2
Group B	11	33	16

The children who gained in rating to a marked extent are characterized by rather uniform behavior on the two occasions, and in only two cases is any rating lower on the second occasion than it was on the first. The children who show a marked loss are characterized by greater variation in behavior. While the number of cases whose behavior ratings on the second test were lower than those on the first is decidedly in excess of that found for Group A, it is noteworthy that this group also includes a greater number of cases whose behavior apparently showed some improvement on the second occasion as compared to the first.

Language handicap.—Improvement in the use of English, consequent upon attendance at an excellent day-nursery, may have been a factor in the increased rating of one child in Group A, who came from a home where a foreign language was used to a considerable extent, though English was also spoken. One or both of the parents was foreign-born in the case of

3 of the children in Group A and 4 of the children in Group B. This is slightly though probably not significantly in excess of the proportion found among the total group of cases studied.

Special physical conditions.—One of the children in Group A had a heavy cold at the time of the first examination, from which he had recovered when the second examination was made. His IQ showed an increase of 27 points. A three-year-old girl had gone without her nap and was reported as being rather cross and irritable at the time of the second examination, which was made in the afternoon while the first had been given in the morning. In spite of this, the second IQ was 35 points higher than the first. A severe cold at the time of the first examination is also recorded for one of the cases in Group B, but although this condition cleared up during the interval between tests, the second IQ was 12 points lower than the first. A boy of 20 months went without his accustomed nap on both occasions; his IQ also shows a loss of 12 points.

No unusual physical conditions are recorded for the remaining cases in these groups. The cases are mentioned, not by way of affording any evidence as to the effect of the physical condition of the subject upon his mental test performance, but rather as illustrations of the misleading effect of basing generalizations upon one or two outstanding examples. It would be easy to impute the marked improvement made by the child first mentioned to the change in his physical condition, but it is less easy to see why a similar improvement in physical status should result in a lowering of the IQ in another case. One is surprised at the marked increase in rating of the child who had missed her nap, but had the conditions chanced to be reversed, so that the low IQ coincided with the omission of the nap, the existence of a causative relationship between the two circumstances might readily have been suspected.

Unreliability of individual tests.—A tabulation was made, showing the number of positive and negative changes in success on each of the individual tests in the scale, occurring within each of the two groups. The results were found to correspond so closely to those given in Table 21 that it seemed not worth while to present them separately. They tend very definitely to confirm the conclusion which might have been drawn from Table 21, that fluctuations in individual performance are not distributed at random over the entire scale, but occur much more frequently in the case of certain tests than with others, and that cases showing extreme changes in IQ tend, upon the whole, to be those in which these changes have chanced to preponderate in one or the other direction.

Marginal successes and failures.—As used here, the term has reference only to those tests which consist of several items, success upon a specified number of which is required for passing. A marginal success is then defined as success upon the required number of items only, the remainder being failed; a marginal failure as success upon one or more items, but not upon a sufficient number to permit credit.

Our data are in certain respects inadequate to determine the precise degree to which marginal scores are responsible for changes in rating, since in many instances only a sufficient number of items were given to determine success or failure on the test in question; while in some cases, especially when the child was unusually difficult to handle, so that pauses for record taking had to be reduced to a minimum, scores were recorded only for the tests *in toto*, no record being made of the separate items. It should be noted further that the standard record blank does not always provide for separate recording of test items.

In spite of the inadequacy of the data, it was possible to

show that marginal scores have figured rather largely in the changes in rating of the two groups of cases under consideration. Tabulation of such data as have been recorded indicates that the ratio of marginal successes to marginal failures made by Group A on the first test is not far from 1 to 3.2, while on the second test the balance shifts so that the ratio becomes approximately 2.8 to 1. The opposite condition is found for Group B. On the first test, marginal success is in excess of marginal failure, while on the second test, failures predominate, but on neither occasion is the recorded ratio as great as 2 to 1. Had all items been recorded, it is entirely probable that the disproportion would have been found to be greater for both groups than is indicated by the foregoing figures. Even as they stand, however, the results are significant, and suggest the desirability of finer calibration of the units of measurement employed.

Failure to gain in mental age during interval between tests.— In order to maintain the IQ at a constant level, one or two more tests should have been passed on the second occasion than on the first, so as to compensate for the increase in chronological age. Three of the fifteen children in Group B passed exactly the same tests on each of the two occasions, with an interval between the two tests of 9 weeks in two cases and 11 weeks in the third case. In three additional cases the loss in rating involved only a single test. It would not, however, be safe to infer that mental growth was actually arrested for a time in these cases. Coarse calibration of the scale, together with unreliability of individual tests, probably constitutes an adequate explanation.

SUMMARY

A comparative study of the data for 14 cases who gained 25 or more points of IQ from first to second test and 15 cases whose IQs dropped 12 points or more tends in general to substantiate the findings reported in the preceding chapters. The group showing marked increases in IQ includes a large percentage of four-year-old children, a slight excess of girls over boys, and is drawn almost entirely from the upper half of the occupational distribution. The group showing marked loss in IQ includes an excess of two-year-old children, almost three times as many boys as girls, and is made up largely of children from the lower half of the occupational distribution. The mean IQs earned on the first test show little difference between the two groups. The data suggest that marginal successes and failures, together with changes in performance upon certain tests previously shown to have low reliability are in the main responsible for these excessive variations. Changes in examiner, language handicaps, the physical condition of the subject, and his behavior during the test, under the conditions of this experiment appear to have been factors of relatively less importance.

CHAPTER VII

DISCUSSION OF RESULTS

Adequacy of the method.—In spite of the care exercised in the selection of cases, and the attempt to maintain control of experimental conditions, the study is still open to criticism from many standpoints. It is believed, nevertheless, that with all its imperfections, it possesses certain points of superiority over others which have been made previously. So far as the writer is aware, the number of cases included is considerably in excess of that reported in any other study dealing with chil-. dren of preschool age. The method of selection of the cases, crude as it is, has the merit of comparative objectivity, and suggests a simple means whereby workers in different communities may compare their standards. It is unquestionably vastly superior to the loose statements as to "selection from an average community," commonly met with in the literature, while the marked differences found to exist between the performances of the children of different occupational groups show beyond reasonable doubt that some kind of experimental control of the selective factor is essential if normative standards are to be free from ambiguity.

In spite of the vast amount of data on retests which has been reported in the literature, one finds comparatively few instances in which either the age of the subjects or the interval between the tests has been treated separately, and still fewer in which both factors have been simultaneously controlled. Since it is entirely possible that variations in mental growth occur more frequently at certain periods than at others, the current practice of treating the length of the interval without reference to the age of the subjects, and vice versa, might easily tend to obscure differences of considerable magnitude. Moreover, since practically all previous reports have been confined to retests made after rather long intervals, it appears highly desirable to compare the findings with those obtained after an interval sufficiently brief to preclude the likelihood of the occurrence of gross changes in actual mental status. It is believed that the present study is the first which has been reported in which the interval between tests has been short enough to permit a comparison of the performance on the separate tests with a view to determining their reliability.

The data on the effect of change in examiner obviously does not warrant wide generalization. Perhaps all that may safely be said is that, provided the examiners are reasonably adept in handling small children and are careful to adhere to a constant procedure throughout, variations in results are not necessarily greater when the retest is made by a different examiner than when it is done by the examiner who gave the first test.

A physical examination given on the same day as the intelligence tests would have been highly desirable. In the absence of this, it is impossible to say what effect varying physical states may have had upon changes in test performance.

Significance of the findings.—There is every reason to believe that the rule of negative acceleration, which has been found characteristic of most growth curves when these are expressed in terms of absolute units of measurement, is applicable also to mental growth. In other words, development probably proceeds more rapidly during the preschool years than at any subsequent period.

If this is true, we must look upon these early years as affording by far the most favorable opportunity for the study of fundamental problems in mental development. It is to be regretted that the widespread interest in intelligence tests as practical devices for social and educational guidance has to some extent caused us to lose sight of their possibilities as research instruments in the field of pure science. It is evident, however, that the tests at present available for use with young children are not sufficiently refined to render them serviceable for use in the solution of problems for which a high degree of precision of measurement is necessary. As a first step toward improvement in method, a critical study of the sources of error in present methods of measurement should be of service. The purpose of the investigation which has been described has been to provide such a study.

While the results obtained may seem somewhat disheartening to the practical worker who has been led to look upon the IQ as an infallible diagnostic measure, the unprejudiced student can hardly fail to read in them much promise for the future. Considering the complexity of the task of mental measurement and the brevity of the period during which it has been studied, the marvel is not that the tests sometimes yield inconsistent results, but that they are so frequently accurate. The fact that almost 4 per cent of our cases showed a change in IQ of 25 points or more within a period of approximately six weeks[1] should point the necessity for considerable caution in interpreting the results of tests given at these early ages. Nevertheless, the obtained correlation of +.81 between original test and retest is surely encouraging. It has been shown that inconsistencies in rating can be traced in large measure to certain of the individual test items. Other important sources of error are marginal successes and failures, incorrect placement of certain tests in the year groups, lack of objectivity in giving or scoring certain items and failure

[1] Of the cases first examined before the age of six years reported by Hildreth in an article on retests with the Stanford Revision, which appeared in the *Pedagogical Seminary and Journal of Genetic Psychology*, September, 1926, more than 7 per cent showed a change of 25 points or more upon a subsequent test.

to secure a maximum response from the child, especially with respect to certain tests which have little intrinsic interest value for children at these ages. Defects of this sort can be corrected. Elimination of unreliable items and substitution of others less subject to modification through chance factors, the use of finer units of measurement, greater precision in the description of procedures and standards, and more consistent attention to the motivating power of the separate items as used with young children should bring about an appreciable improvement in the reliability of the scale.

The IQ and prediction.—Previous studies in mental development, and especially those dealing with the constancy of the IQ have demonstrated that the following hypotheses may be considered reasonably sound:

1. Apart from pathological conditions, mental growth already accomplished will not be lost before the onset of senescence.

2. Mental growth is confined to a limited period of life. The exact boundaries of this period have not been determined, and it is probable that there is some individual variation in this respect. The limiting factor appears to be more nearly a function of chronological age than of mental age.

These studies have also shown that in the case of school children, a very high correlation exists between the intelligence quotients earned on two tests by the same individual, even though the tests are separated by a period of several years. This has been interpreted by many as meaning that the mean increment of mental growth during the interval is, within the limits of chance error, exactly proportional to the mean rate of mental growth previous to the first examination, i.e., to the IQ earned at that time. That a general tendency in this direction exists is probably true, but it must not be forgotten that a high correlation between first test and retest is to be expected purely upon the basis of the two propositions which have just been stated, even though there were no relationship between rate of growth previous to the first examination and subsequent rate; inasmuch as the status at the time of the second test includes the status at the time of the first test, plus an increment. Suppose, for example, that a group of children were examined at the age of nine years and again at the age of twelve. Suppose, furthermore, that at the time of the first examination, the IQs were found to range from 50 to 150, the mental ages from four and a half to thirteen and a half, but that during the three-year interval all the children gained exactly three years mentally. Under those circumstances the IQ would have no predictive value as far as ensuing mental growth is concerned, but the correlation between first and second tests would still be high. The children who formerly rated at 150 would have dropped to 138.5; those at 50 would have increased to 62.5, while the intermediate cases would show a correspondingly smaller change. Given a perfectly reliable measurement on both occasions, and allowing equal weight to each year's growth, the theoretical correlation would be approximately .866. Unreliability of measurement would, of course, lower this figure.

From a practical standpoint we are entirely justified in the statement that the IQ earned on a single test has high predictive value in the case of school children, provided that it is clearly understood that this prediction (if based upon the correlation between retests) has reference to future status rather than to future rate of growth, since it is the former rather than the latter in which we are usually interested. Moreover, common sense would lead us to expect that if retardation or acceleration is not the result of pure chance, some degree of correlation between earlier and later rates of growth would ordinarily be found, since our social organization is such that the factors determining growth-rate would be more likely to remain somewhat similar than to become radically different. That some correlation between past rate of growth and rate of increment does exist is evident from the data reported in the literature; that this correlation is appreciably lower than that between the IQs found at two successive stages can also be shown empirically as well as theoretically.

The bearing of this upon the question of intelligence testing during the preschool period is obvious. If the period of mental growth has been in large measure accomplished, then the essential point is that the degree of mental development which has been already attained shall be established with accuracy. Since the remaining increment is in any case small, an error in predicting its amount is of relatively less consequence. If, however, the measurement is taken early in life, when the major portion of postnatal growth is still to be accomplished, the question of prediction is on a very different footing. It is doubtful whether any of the data which have been published up to the present time are adequate to show to what extent an IQ earned before the age of six yars is predictive of adult mental status. It is very probable that even were such a measurement absolutely accurate at the time of testing, its predictive value would still be considerably lower than an equally accurate measurement taken at the age of twelve. Further evidence, in which the effect of varying intervals between tests is treated with reference to the age at the time of the first test, is needed.

There seems to be no valid reason why it should not be possible to develop a series of tests which would measure intellectual status as accurately at the age of two years as at twelve or fourteen. Such a method would constitute a most important contribution to psychological technique—a contribution which should not be evaluated solely on the basis of its possibilities for social and educational prediction. If the measurement makes possible an accurate expression of the child's mental status at the time, its value as a scientific instrument is assured. Even from the strictly pragmatic viewpoint, it is perhaps as profitable to direct our energies toward a study of mental progress from year to year under varying conditions as to attempt to predict the college grades to be earned by our two-year-olds sixteen years hence. There are many problems both directly and indirectly related to the field of mental growth which could be approached most profitably during the early years of life when both mental and physical growth are proceeding at a maximum rate. The need of a more reliable method of measurement is very evident.

The objection may, of course, be raised that since this study has dealt only with the Kuhlman Revision of the Binet, any conclusions based upon the results are of necessity limited to this particular scale, and that if a different scale had been used, the results might have been more favorable. The first statement is beyond question true; the second is very doubtful. A survey of the tests suitable for use with children of preschool age reveals only three composite scales which are applicable to children as young as two years. These are the Kuhlman Revision of the Binet, Gesell's new series of tests, and the Stutsman Scale of Performance Tests. The Gesell series is highly suggestive for future work, but in its present form it makes no pretence of affording more than a very rough classification; while for the Stutsman series the only norms thus far published are percentile scores for the various tests separately, with no method of arriving at a combined score. It might be added that the materials for neither the Gesell nor the Stutsman series had been placed on the market at the time this study was begun. It appears, therefore, that the choice of tests was as wise as could have been made. While the results show that a child's performance on this test does not afford a sufficient basis for any final or dogmatic statements as to his developmental status, they also show that in the great majority of cases the test results are far too consistent to be the result of chance, and that upon the whole a considerable degree of reliance may be placed upon them. It is believed that this study has fulfilled its purpose to the extent that it has been able to point out certain elements of weakness in the scale as it stands, and to suggest means for their correction. Upon the basis of these findings, a tentative revision and expansion of the scale is now being tried out. This revision includes two forms of comparable difficulty, and is planned to have a range of usefulness extending from eighteen months up to six years.

APPENDIX A

COMPOSITION OF OCCUPATIONAL CATEGORIES[1]

GROUP I

Architects	114
Civil engineers and surveyors	223
Clergymen	179
College presidents and professors	231
Dentists	321
Editors and reporters	95
Electrical and mechanical engineers	227
Lawyers, judges and justices	480
Musicians and teachers of music	318
Physicians and surgeons	409
Teachers (Unclassified)	280
All other professions	802
Total	3,679
Per cent of total population	5.4

GROUP II

Managers and superintendents (mfg.)	1,005
Manufacturers	502
Officials (mfg.)	253
Officials and superintendents (railroad)	120
Bankers and bank officials	191
Commercial brokers and commission men	162
Proprietors, officials and managers, n. o. s.*	285
Stock brokers	222
Wholesale dealers, importers and exporters	323

* "Not otherwise stated."

[1] Based upon total male population of Minneapolis, 1920, between ages 21-45.

Hotel keepers and managers 118
Accountants and auditors 646
Draftsmen 201
Photographers 111
Officials and inspectors, state and U. S. 173

Total 4,312
Per cent of total population 6.3

GROUP III

Officials and inspectors, city and county 91
Compositors, linotypers, and typesetters 587
Railroad mail clerks 181
Telegraph operators 111
Commercial travelers 1,655
Floorwalkers and foremen in stores 114
Insurance agents 496
Real estate agents and officials 636
Retail dealers 3,084
Sales agents 250
"All other occupations" public service 172
Restaurant, cafe, and lunchroom keepers 184
Bookkeepers and cashiers 1,208
Stenographers and typists 104
"All other occupations" agriculture, forestry, and animal
    husbandry 256
Builders and building contractors 359
Cabinet makers 286
Carpenters 359
Electricians 286
Stationary engineers 2,891
Foremen and overseers (mfg.) 841
Jewelers, lapidaries, and watchmakers 651
Machinists 755
Mechanics 122
Millers 3,719
Millwrights 375
Plumbers, gas and steam fitters 780
Pressmen and plate printers 145

Conductors (steam railroad)	255
Inspectors (steam railroad)	169
Locomotive engineers	494
Clerks in stores	592
Clerks, not in stores	3,411
Collectors	79
Total	25,698
Per cent of total population	37.3

GROUP IV

Mail carriers	216
Inspectors, gaugers, and samplers	115
Salesmen in stores	4,458
"All other occupations" under trade	626
Policemen	172
Agents	766
Canvassers	44
Farmers	147
Bakers	310
Blacksmiths	338
Boilermakers	270
Brick and stone masons	396
Coopers	71
Iron molders, founders, and casters	298
Painters, glaziers, and varnishers (not in factory)	1,051
Painters, glaziers, and varnishers (in factory)	276
Plasterers and cement finishers	299
Shoemakers and cobblers	184
Tailors	470
Tinsmiths and sheet-metal workers	375
Upholsterers	167
"All other occupations" under manufacturing	949
Conductors, street railroad	449
Foremen and overseers, transportation	299
Locomotive firemen	413
Motormen, street railway	509
"All other occupations" transportation	811
Chauffeurs	665

Apprentices to building and hand trades	17
Firemen (city fire department)	329
Barbers, hair dressers, and manicurists	618
Waiters	438
Telegraph and telephone linemen	216
Total	16,762
Per cent of total population	24.3

GROUP V

Messenger, bundle, and office boys	19
Extraction of minerals (all occupations)	81
Firemen, n. o. s.	326
Semi-skilled operatives, n. o. s.	4,349
Brakemen	363
Draymen, teamsters, and expressmen	1,309
Switchmen and flagmen	698
Deliverymen	755
Newsboys	19
Guards, watchmen, and doorkeepers	82
Elevator tenders	112
Janitors and sextons	404
Laundry operatives	143
Porters	328
Servants	748
All other occupations, domestic and personal service	557
Total	10,293
Per cent of total population	14.9

GROUP VI

Laborers, farm	672
Laborers, manufacturing	4,661
Laborers, transportation	1,559
Laborers, trade	981
Laborers, public service	320
Total	8,193
Per cent of total population	11.8

COMBINED ENVELOPE FILE AND EXAMINER'S GUIDE FOR USE IN GIVING THE KUHLMAN-BINET TESTS

The following section describes the method of constructing the envelope file referred to in Chapter II. For the convenience of those who are using the scale for the examination of older children as well as those of preschool age, directions for the complete file, which provides for all the material used throughout the scale, have been included.

The advantages of this system of assembling the material will be obvious to anyone who has ever attempted to use these tests. The complete series involves the use of 112 different cards of several different sizes and shapes, and of 11 different kinds of printed forms, also of varied sizes, besides the set of weights and the various small objects used at the lower age-levels. Even when all testing is done in a single laboratory where the plan of arrangement can be kept more nearly constant, occasional misplacements are likely to occur, while in the case of the examiner who goes from school to school, taking his material with him, the need for some permanent assembling of the various items becomes manifest.

An additional source of difficulty in giving this test is to be found in the extremely abbreviated record form used, which necessitates continued reference to the manual of directions. Although it is undoubtedly true, as Dr. Kuhlman points out, that reference to the manual rather than reliance upon the memory has the advantage of assuring a more uniform procedure in giving the tests, it is also true that a shy, nervous, or timid child is likely to be made quite ill at ease by having the examiner read all his questions out of a book.

The method of arranging the material about to be described not only has the advantage of permanent assembling, thus doing away with delays in locating the items as needed, but also provides the examiner with a guide for procedure to which he can refer easily and naturally without the subject becoming aware that he is doing so.

The plan provides for a separate envelope of suitable size to contain the cards or other forms used for each test of the scale. The directions for giving and scoring the test (as given in the manual) are printed on the outside of each envelope. Holes are punched in the margins, and by this means the envelopes are bound together with tape in the form of a large book. Substantial board covers are added for protection. The fastening should be sufficiently loose so that the envelopes when filled can still be turned readily as the pages of a book are turned.

In giving the tests, the open book is placed on the table at the examiner's right, the subject being seated at the left. As the tests are given, the examiner is able to refer casually to the directions as he takes the materials from the envelopes. When several cards are used for a single test, each one is placed on the table face downward as it is used, thus keeping the order undisturbed. Since the envelopes are of a size which fits the cards, this order will be maintained when the material is not in use. All material should be replaced as it is used, thus keeping the file always in readiness for the next test.

The entire outfit should be provided with a pair of carrying straps and handles. These are very inexpensive and can be obtained at any stationery or luggage shop. The straps should be long enough to permit the inclusion of a box containing the set of weights and other small articles used in the test. This constitutes a portable testing outfit, which is always ready for use.

The following outline gives the dimensions of the different parts of the file, and indicates the arrangement of the contents and placement of the directions for administering and scoring the tests. In the sets used at the Institute, these directions have been typed on separate sheets, which were then pasted in place. The references are to the pages of the manual mentioned before.

Item	Size	Contents	Test directions to be placed on front of envelope.
2 heavy cards	13″ by 11″	....	Tests for ages 3 mo. to 18 mo. inc. (pp. 86-93).
Envelope No. 1	6½″ by 11″	Record blanks	"Scores required for passing" (sheet furnished with equipment).
Envelope No. 2	6½″ by 11″	Cards for II 1	Tests for age 2. (pp. 93-94).
Envelope No. 3	8½″ by 11″	Cards for III 1 and VII 1	Tests III 1 (p. 95), VII 1 (p. 109), III 2, III 3, III 4, III 5, III 6 (pp. 95-96).
Envelope No. 4	4″ by 6″	Cards for III 7	Test III 7 (pp. 96-97).
Envelope No. 5	6½″ by 11″	Sheets for III 8	Test III 8 (pp. 97-98).
Envelope No. 6	6½″ by 11″	Card for IV 3 Sheets for IV 5	Tests IV 1, IV 2, IV 3 IV 5 (pp. 98-99).
Envelope No. 7	13″ by 11″	Large cards for IV 4 and IV 6	Tests IV 4 (pp. 98-99) and IV 6 (p. 100).
Envelope No. 8	4″ by 6″	Small cards for IV 4	....
Envelope No. 9	4″ by 6″	Small cards for IV 6	Test IV 7 (p. 100).
Envelope No. 10	4″ by 6″	Cards for IV 8	Test IV 8 (pp. 100-101)
Envelope No. 11	4″ by 6″ (With string fastener)	Coins for V 1 and VII 2	Test V 1, (p. 101) and VII 2 (p. 109).
Envelope No. 12	4″ by 6″	Cards for V 2	Test V 2 (pp. 101-102)
Envelope No. 13	4″ by 6″	Cards for V 4	Tests V 3, V 4 (pp. 102-103).
Envelope No. 14	6½″ by 11″	Cards for V 8	Tests V 5, V 6, V 7, and V 8 (pp. 103-104)
Envelope No. 15	6½″ by 11″	Cards for VI 2	Tests VI 1, VI 2, VI 3 (pp. 104-105).
Envelope No. 16	6½″ by 11″	Cards for VI 4	Tests VI 4, VI 5, VI 6 (pp. 105-107).

Item	Size	Contents	Test directions to be placed on front of envelope.
Envelope No. 17	6½" by 11"	Sheets for VI 7	Tests VI 7, VI 8 (pp. 107-108).
Heavy card	6½" by 11"	....	Test VII 1 "See Envelope No. 3." Test VII 2 "See Envelope No. 11." Tests VII 3, VIII 4, VII 5, VII 6 (pp. 109-111).
Envelope No. 18	6½" by 11"	Cards for VII 8 and VIII 1	Tests VII 7, VII 8, VIII 1 (pp. 111-112).
Envelope No. 19	13" by 11"	Sheets for VIII 4	Tests VIII 2, VIII 3, VIII 4, VIII 5, VIII 6 (pp. 112-116).
Envelope No. 20	6½" by 11"	Sheets for VIII 7	Test VIII 7 (pp. 116-117).
Envelope No. 21	6½" by 11"	Cards for VIII 8 (IX 8, X 2)	Test VIII 8 (pp. 117-118).
Envelope No. 22	13" by 11"	Sheets for IX 6	Tests IX 1 to IX 7 inc. (pp. 118-122). Test IX 8 "See Envelope No. 21."
Envelope No. 23	6½" by 11"	Cards for X 1	Test X 1 (p. 123). Test X 2 "See Envelope No. 21." Test X 3 (XII 1), X 4 (pp. 124-125).
Envelope No. 24	6½" by 11"	Cards for X 6 (XI 4, XII 2)	Tests X 5, X 6 (pp. 125-127).
Envelope No. 25	6½" by 11"	Cards for X 7 (XI 5, XII 3)	Test X 7 (pp. 127-128)
Envelope No. 26	6½" by 11"	Cards for X 8 (XI 7, XII 5, XIII-XV 2)	Test X 8 (pp. 128-129)
Envelope No. 27	6½" by 11"	Cards for XI 1	Tests XI 1, XI 2, and XI 3 (pp. 129-130). Test XI 4 "See Envelope No. 24." Test XI 5 "See Envelope No. 25."
Envelope No. 28	6½" by 11"	Sheets and key card for XI 6 (XII 4, XIII-XV 1)	Test XI 6 (p. 133). Test XI 7 "See Envelope No. 26."

Item	Size	Contents	Test directions to be placed on front of envelope.
Envelope No. 29	8½″ by 11″	Sheets for XI 8 (XII 6 XIII-XV 3)	Test XI 8 (pp. 134-135).
Envelope No. 30	4″ by 6″	Small cards for XI 8 (XII 6, XIII-XV 3)	....
Envelope No. 31	6½″ by 11″	Sheets for XII 7 (XIII-XV 4)	Test XII 1 "See Envelope No. 23." Test XII 2 "See Envelope No. 24." Test XII 3 "See Envelope No. 25." Test XII 4 "See Envelope No. 28." Test XII 5 "See Envelope No. 26." Test XII 6 "See Envelopes No. 29-30." Test XII 7 (p. 140).
Envelope No. 32	6½″ by 11″	Sheets and cards for XIII-XV 6	Tests XIII-XV 6 (pp. 146-147).
Envelope No. 33	13″ by 11″	Sheets and cards for XII 8 (XIII-XV 5)	Test XII 8 (pp. 140-141). Test XIII-XV 1 "See Envelope No. 28." Test XIII-XV 2 "See Envelope No. 26." Test XIII-XV 3 "See Envelopes No. 29-30." Test XIII-XV 4 "See Envelope No. 31." Test XIII-XV 5 "See above."
Envelope No. 34	6½″ by 11″	Sheets and cards for XIII-XV 7	Test XIII-XV 7 (pp. 147-148).
Envelope No. 35	6½″ by 11″	Cards for XIII-XV 8	Test XIII-XV 8 (pp. 148-149).
Heavy card	13″ by 11″	....	"Rules for determining mental age" (pp. 80-81). "Determining the grade of intelligence" (p. 82).

SUMMARY OF MATERIAL REQUIRED

2 heavy covers, size 12″ by 15″, punched alike as follows: 6 holes at 2″ intervals 1″ from margin on one of the 15″ sides. One hole ½″ from margin in center of each of the three remaining sides. (Short lengths of tape passed through the center holes and tied provide against any possibility of loss of material in transportation.)

4 manilla envelopes, size 13″ by 11″ without flaps, open on long side, each punched with 6 holes at 2″ intervals ½″ from margin on side opposite open side.

3 bristol-board cards, size 13″ by 11″ punched as above.

21 manilla envelopes, size 6½″ by 11″ without flaps, open on short side, each punched with 3 holes at 2″ intervals ½″ from margin on side opposite open side.

1 bristol-board card, size 6½″ by 11″, punched as above.

2 manilla envelopes, size 8½″ by 11″ without flaps, open on short side, 4 holes punched at 2″ intervals ½″ from margin on side opposite open end.

7 manilla envelopes, size 4″ by 6″ without flaps, open on short side, 2 holes punched at 2″ intervals ½″ from margin on side opposite open end.

1 manilla envelope, size 4″ by 6″, with flap and substantial string fastening, punched same as above.

Envelopes should be made of heavy manilla cardboard or oak tag. In assembling the file, it should be noted that a single "page" is made up of either one 13″ by 11″ envelope or card, two of size 6½″ by 11″, laid side by side, three of the 4″ by 6″ size, or one 8½″ by 11″ with one 4″ by 6″.

INDEX